COOKING
FOR YOUR
BABY
THE
NATURAL
WAY

COOKING FOR YOUR BABY THE NATURAL WAY

LARAINE TOMS

 Sterling Publishing Co. Inc. New York

Library of Congress Cataloging in Publication Data

Toms, Laraine.
  Cooking for your baby the natural way.

  Includes index.
  1. Cookery (Baby foods)   2. Cookery (Natural foods)
I. Title.
TX740.T65   1984   641.5'622   83-24108
ISBN 0-8069-7826-0 (pbk.)

Copyright © 1984, 1978 by Laraine Toms
American edition published in 1984 by Sterling Publishing Co., Inc.
Two Park Avenue, New York, N.Y. 10016
First edition published in Australia in 1978 by
Thomas Nelson Australia, 480 Latrobe Street, Melbourne 3000
Manufactured in the United States of America

CONTENTS

For Christopher and David

INTRODUCTION

Parents are generally agreed on what they want most for their children. To be happy, to be confident and well-loved, to be successful and, most of all, to be healthy and strong. Yet so many of these same parents are unwittingly starting their children's lives with a handicap, reducing each child's potential for full development because of poor nutrition in early infancy and childhood. Few of our children are hungry—indeed most are overfed—but are they given the right health-building, natural foods to ensure proper growth and robust health for a lifetime?

I have written this book because I believe that there is a need to point out to other mothers that there is an alternative to precooked, commercial baby food; that their reliance on jars and cans is, in fact, selling their babies short. I have children too. I know only too well how each day seems crammed to the limit and how tempting it is to reach for those "convenience" foods so attractively displayed and convincingly advertised. But, in fact, very little extra effort is required to prepare good food for your own baby; it can be a creative, satisfying experience and the rewards are immense.

Lifelong food habits are formed in infancy and childhood. The foods introduced early usually become favorites for life. There are too many future obese adults in training, babies being brought up on too much starch and white sugar, overrefined flour and cereals, overprocessed, vitamin-reduced food. The right diet from the very beginning can reduce the likelihood of your child suffering from obesity and heart disease in adulthood. Take a good look at the labels of those cans of commercial baby food; see how large a proportion of that meat and vegetable dinner is made up of nutritionless "fillers"—starches and sugar. How much chicken is in the chicken purée? Of equal concern are the additives and the high level of salt found in canned baby food, a taste geared to please mother, and not in the best interests of the baby. Three major manufacturers of canned or bottled baby food have recently ceased to add salt to their products.

Recent research on the hyperactive child has led doctors to look carefully at food additives found in the diets of young children. We read also of too-fat babies, of unfit children, problems which could have been avoided with a simple, natural diet.

At this point I feel I must say clearly that commercial baby food can serve a useful purpose in helping mothers through emergencies, and those unbelievably chaotic days that we all suffer. But let's not rely on them to the exclusion of freshly cooked, natural food.

This book is a light-hearted attempt to introduce you to the joys of making your own baby food, from homemade yogurt to baby casseroles, snacks and ice cream.

Let's build health—what greater head start can we give our children?

1
BUT I
DON'T HAVE
MUCH TIME

Preparing your own baby food takes much less time and effort and is far simpler than you might think. Babies aren't gourmets; they don't need four-course banquets of exotic ingredients—they thrive on fresh, natural food, simply prepared and served with a minimum of fuss.

Basically, baby will eat what the rest of the family eats so there is no need for special shopping excursions for baby food ingredients—base baby's menu on the family's meals to save yourself time and money.

Naturally, you won't have the time, nor will you want to spend hours each day preparing baby food. Of course, freshly prepared food served immediately is best, but this just isn't possible every day. Instead of relying on cans and jars of commercial baby food, it is far better to prepare certain foods, such as meat and vegetable purées, stewed fruits, soups and stocks, in large quantities and freeze them for later use. One good way of freezing baby food is the ice cube tray method. Pour purée, soups or fruit into ice cube trays, freeze, then store the cubes in freezer bags for later use. Complete meals of mixed meat and vegetable purée, yogurt and fruit or soup can be frozen in small plastic containers, and are especially good when you want to go out for the day, or for traveling. Babies aren't fussy about the temperature of their food. Meat and vegetable purée served at room temperature tastes just as good to them as if it were warmed. Stocks and meat purées should be thawed in the refrigerator, as these foods are an excellent breeding ground for bacteria.

Do try to make the most of the time you spend in the kitchen. Have several things cooking at once, such as a beef stew, apples and a big pot of stock. If you have to stand with an eagle eye over the custard, why not watch a batch of biscuits or a roast at the same time?

Make as much use as possible of those natural convenience foods, yogurt and eggs. Make you own yogurt; it's simple to prepare, economical and stores well. Fruit and yogurt make a meal, so serve it often as a lunch for babies and toddlers; it takes no more time to spoon yogurt and fruit into a dish than it does to open a can of baby food and heat it. Eggs are versatile and wonderful time-savers—they don't even have to be cooked! Whipped up with fruit juice or milk, they provide a meal in a minute.

Of course, when you first begin, making your own baby food will involve time and effort. It will take a little while before you start thinking in terms of baby portions of the roast, saving leftover vegetables from the family's meal, cooking larger quantities for freezing, etc., but once you are organized you will find the little extra time involved is so worthwhile for the better health and vitality you will be giving your child, and the satisfaction you, as a responsible parent, will feel.

2
WHAT
WILL I NEED?

Basic equipment needed for preparation and storage of baby's food

You probably already have most of the utensils needed to prepare baby food quickly and easily. Saucepans, a colander, a grater, measuring cups and spoons, a spatula—these are basic items found in most kitchens. However, there are a few extra items which you might not have now but which will make baby food preparation so much easier.

The first of these are the *electric blender* and the *food processor*—for me, the most valuable appliances in my kitchen. Although the initial cost is quite high, the savings to you in both time and money are incalculable. Not only will you save time and money in preparing baby food but you will find a thousand uses for your blender or processor in preparing food for the whole family. They are great aids to better nutrition for everyone. Soups, drinks, fruit desserts, main courses, all using fresh, natural ingredients, are so easy to prepare. Best of all, once you own one you will be far less tempted to use canned and processed baby foods for "convenience"—making your own is no effort at all.

A cheaper alternative to the above is the *mouli*. This sieves, purées and grates most foods with very little effort, and if you buy one with several interchangeable grating discs, it will have many uses in general cooking as well as in preparing baby foods.

Another invaluable kitchen utensil is the *steamer basket*. Your aim in preparing your own baby's food will be to preserve the natural vitamins and minerals. One of the best methods of cooking vegetables is to steam them in a metal basket inside or on top of a tightly covered saucepan, above rapidly

boiling water. By cooking vegetables this way, many of the nutrients which are water soluble are not lost in the cooking water. A collapsible steamer basket which fits most sizes of saucepans is readily available in most supermarkets and hardware stores. Your whole family will enjoy steamed vegetables as they really do have a better flavor and color. The water left after cooking vegetables this way can be used to purée other baby foods or to make soup, or it can be given to baby in his bottle instead of plain water.

A *fine mesh strainer* (preferably nylon) is important for straining milk and fruit drinks into bottles and cups.

Instead of peeling carrots and potatoes, scrub them with a *vegetable brush*—a nailbrush will do. Use it to clean thoroughly all raw fruits and vegetables.

An electric juicer is expensive, and definitely an optional extra, but a *hand juicer* is essential for fresh orange juice.

You will need *ice cube trays* for freezing baby-sized portions of puréed meat, vegetables and fruit, and plastic freezer bags to store the frozen cubes.

Small glass or plastic *containers* with tight sealing lids, which can be stored in both ordinary and freezer sections of your refrigerator, are really useful—you will probably need six or so of these. They are great for storing leftovers or baby-sized meals as they keep food fresh and nutritious. When using glass, remember to allow room for the expansion occurring when liquids freeze.

Plastic bags are useful for storing playdough in the refrigerator and for keeping vegetables crisp, but please take care to puncture several large holes in *any* plastic bag you keep—the danger of suffocation for small children is very real and can so easily be avoided.

3
FIRST SOLIDS—
FRUIT
AND FRUIT JUICE

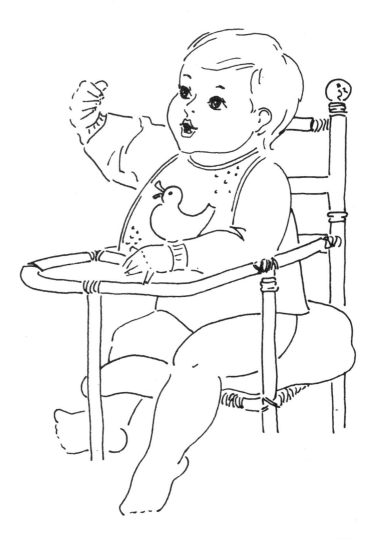

You probably have your own ideas about the best time to introduce your baby to solid foods. Your baby doctor will also advise on what, when, and how much. However, for convenience the order which I have found works well is:

1. Mashed ripe banana
2. Scraped apple or applesauce
3. Yogurt
4. First vegetables—sweet potato and carrots
5. Cereals
6. Egg yolk. This is introduced at around six months because of its high iron content. Until they are six months old babies have sufficient iron stored in their bodies, but after this time they need to include iron-rich foods in their diet
7. Other vegetables
8. White meat—chicken, fish
9. Variety meat—brains and liver
10. Red meat—veal, beef, lamb

Fruit can make an excellent introduction to solid food for your baby. You have probably been giving him or her orange juice from around the age of 3–5 weeks, so what could be more natural than to progress to fruit for baby's first solid food experience? Choose the fruits carefully and always buy fruit in season, making sure it is thoroughly ripe and sound. *As with any new food, introduce fruits slowly, one at a time, beginning with just a taste and gradually increasing the quantity daily if your baby doesn't show any allergic reaction.*

As well as the old faithfuls, apples and bananas, try offering other fresh fruits in season. But use some caution. Berries have seeds which very young babies are not equipped to handle, and they may cause a rash if introduced too early. Citrus fruits are a common cause of allergy when given to tiny babies, so introduce these carefully. Begin with 1 teaspoon orange juice in 8 teaspoons of boiled water, gradually increasing the quantity of juice. Do avoid canned fruits, both those especially for babies, and others, as they contain large quantities of sugar. However, baby strained fruits in cans and carefully drained canned fruits are better than no fruits at all!

When fresh fruits are scarce, for babies about 6 months, place prunes and dried apricots in a glass jar, cover with water and leave overnight, then steam them the next day and purée.

Fruits make excellent finger foods for babies learning to feed themselves. Try a peeled banana or slices of pear or peach. Avoid hard fruits as these can choke very young children.

Drinks made with fresh fruit and juices, milk, honey, and even cheese are delicious and can be enjoyed by the whole family. From baby's first spoonful of orange juice in boiled water to the most wildly imaginative fruit and yogurt blend for older children, fruit drinks are for health plus!

Instead of buying bottled sweet sauces for ice cream, make your own delicious, nutritious fruit toppings.

BANANAS

Bananas make a wonderful first solid food, but make sure they are thoroughly ripe with brown markings. When ripe, bananas are easy for baby to digest and are packed with vitamins and minerals. Their natural sweetness baby will love; no need to add sugar or honey.

For babies from four months old, simply peel a ripe banana and mash a little of it, mixing in some milk or water to make it very liquid for their first attempts at solids. When your baby is enjoying bananas straight, you can use them as a "mixer," perhaps in the following ways.

BANANA YOGURT
4 months

A great favorite. Just mix mashed banana with plain, Homemade Yogurt. Kids of all ages love this. Try freezing banana yogurt in ice cube trays with ice cream sticks for the over-ones.

BANANA APPLES
4 months

Mix mashed banana with stewed or freshly grated apple.
Bananas can be mixed with any fruits in season.

BANANA EGG
6 months

½ *banana*
½ *hard-cooked egg yolk*

This is a good way to introduce eggs into baby's diet. Make sure the egg is hard-cooked and use *only* the yolk. For the first taste, begin by mixing just a tiny amount (less than ¼ teaspoon) of egg yolk with the banana; gradually increase the amount of egg until a whole yolk is used.

BANANA AND COTTAGE CHEESE
6 months

The whole family will enjoy this one.

½ cup cottage cheese
½ cup mashed banana
4 tablespoons fresh orange juice
1 teaspoon honey

Mix all ingredients thoroughly and serve at once. Try mixing other fresh fruits with cottage cheese, too: puréed mango or pineapple, freshly grated apple, or mashed melon. All delicious.

APPLES

Apples also make an ideal first food for babies and will often be firm favorites well past childhood.

APPLE JUICE
4 months

6 apples—use Jonathans if making
juice for the very young; older babies
and children will enjoy juice made
from all varieties of apples

Wash the apples and chop roughly; there is no need to peel or core them. Simmer gently in 6 cups water for 15–20 minutes. Strain, and pour into containers.

SCRAPED APPLE (OR PEAR)
4 months

When introducing your baby to raw apples, choose only ripe eating apples— Jonathans or Delicious. Scrape some raw apple with a spoon and put a little of it in the baby's mouth. Start with ¼ teaspoon, gradually increasing it. When your baby is sitting in his high chair, give him a mound of grated apple to experiment with.

APPLESAUCE
4 months

Any variety of apples may be stewed. Wash, core, and peel apples thinly; slice and put into saucepan with just enough water to cover the base. Cook gently for 10 minutes until apples are soft but not mushy. Purée in blender or through mouli for the very young; mash with a fork for older babies and children. Don't add sugar! If the apples are very sour, add a little honey after they are cooked. Serve with yogurt, custard, cottage cheese, or blended with other fruits and vegetables.

PURÉED APPLE, RAW
4 months

It's a good idea to prepare large quantities of puréed apple, raw or cooked, and freeze for use on busy days.

peeled and cored raw apples (red eating
    apples)
homemade Apple Juice

Slice apples, place in blender with juice, then blend until smooth.

BAKED APPLE
12 months

1 red eating apple
1 teaspoon honey
a little butter
cinnamon, nutmeg (for older children)

Wash, dry and core apple a little more than halfway through. Fill cavity with honey, butter and spices. Slit the skin around the center of the apple to prevent it from bursting, then place in a small dish with just a little water in the bottom to prevent it from sticking. Bake in a moderate oven until soft.

DRINKS AND TOPPINGS

PINEAPPLE DELIGHT
5 months

1 slice fresh pineapple
1 cup orange juice
½ banana
honey to taste

Blend, then strain into bottles or cups.

CARROT JUICE
5 months

1 lb. carrots
4 cups water
½ cup nonfat dry milk

Wash and scrape carrots and cut into small pieces. Place all the ingredients in a tightly covered saucepan and bring to a boil. Simmer for 1 hour. Cool and strain. Store in an airtight container in the refrigerator or freeze.

APPLE LEMONADE
6 months

1 cup Apple Juice
2 tablespoons lemon juice
2 teaspoons honey
½ cup freshly grated apple

Blend. Strain into bottle or cup for the very young.

APPLE SHAKES
6 months

Blend 1 cup Apple Juice with any fruits in season; add honey to taste if needed. A tablespoon of nonfat dry milk adds protein and variety to apple shakes.

CAROB MILK
8 months

Carob is available at health food stores and makes an excellent chocolate substitute for all age groups. It is naturally sweet, rather like chocolate, but rich in calcium, potassium, and phosphorus.

1 cup milk
2 teaspoons carob powder

Blend together.

BANANA DELIGHT
8 months

For busy days, misery days and days when you just can't be bothered.

1 cup milk
1 ripe banana
1 egg
1 teaspoon honey

Blend and strain into a bottle or cup for an instant complete meal. *Omit the egg for babies not yet taking raw egg or use only the raw yolk.*

FRUITY MILK SHAKE

Blend 1 cup milk with any of the following fruits: apple, pear, peach, or pineapple.

YOGURT FRUIT SHAKE
8 months

1 cup plain Yogurt
1 cup orange juice
1 ripe banana
1 tablespoon honey

Blend and strain into baby's bottle.

BANANA SMOOTHIE
9 months

1½ cups fresh orange juice
1 large banana
1 teaspoon honey

Blend, strain, and pour into baby's bottle and into glasses for the rest of the family. Delicious with a little mint, too.

ORANGEADE OR LEMONADE
12 months

2 lemons or oranges
½ cup honey
2½ cups water

Wash fruit well. Do not peel. Cut into small pieces, removing the seeds. Place all ingredients in blender and blend for 5 minutes. Strain and chill.

HONEYED LEMONADE
12 months

A great winter's day warmer.

1½ cups honey
1 cup fresh lemon juice
5 cups water
mint leaves

Mix all ingredients together in a saucepan, over low heat. Don't overheat, as this destroys the vitamin C.

LEMONADE
12 months

4–6 lemons
6 cups water
1½ cups raw sugar

Peel the rind from lemons as thinly as possible, discarding any pith. Put rinds into a saucepan with 2 cups water and the sugar. Simmer gently for 15 minutes. Strain and cool. Squeeze enough lemons to make 1 cup juice and strain into a large pitcher. Add remaining 4 cups water and cooled syrup. Chill.

APRICOT TOPPING
12 months

You can prepare other fruit toppings in the same way, using fresh or dried fruit.

8 oz. dried apricots
water to cover
2–3 tablespoons honey

Soak apricots overnight. Next day, simmer apricots gently till tender, then stir in honey. Remove apricots with a slotted spoon and purée in blender till smooth. Return to cooking liquid; stir over low heat until well mixed. Check consistency; if too thick, add more water.

BLENDER GOODIES

If you have a blender (or food processor) you can make many interesting health-building drinks for the whole family. Try some of the following combinations:

1 cup unsweetened pineapple juice plus 1 tablespoon cottage cheese
1 cup orange juice plus 1 tablespoon cream cheese
1 cup orange juice plus 1 egg yolk
1 cup unsweetened pineapple juice plus ½ cup freshly grated coconut, all strained.

Invent your own combinations, using orange juice as a base with chunks of fresh fruit, yogurt, honey, or cheese additions.

Note: 1 tablespoon of plain yogurt added to any fruit or milk beverage is a nutritional plus!

4
YOGURT

Make yogurt a basic food for your whole family. Whole-milk yogurt makes an excellent first food for babies, so from 4–5 months it could be included in baby's diet every day. Because yogurt is more easily digested than the milk from which it is made, even completely breast-fed babies find it easy to digest, and it's a great way to gradually introduce them to cow's milk. It also has a greater concentration of B complex vitamins than whole milk.

Yogurt is a wonderful convenience food for babies and children and a quick lunch for moms who don't have time to prepare themselves a proper meal. Use it as a mixer with fruit and vegetables and serve with wheat germ and fruit for a quick, nutritious breakfast or lunch.

And make your own yogurt. It's easy, economical and you can be sure there are no added sugars. Any kind of milk can be used—whole milk, skim milk, nonfat dry milk, evaporated milk, even soybean milk.

The bacteria live on the sugar in the milk and break it down into lactic acid which causes the milk to curdle and become like junket. As soon as the yogurt is the right "thickness," it must be placed in the refrigerator, where the coldness stops the further growth of bacteria and prevents the yogurt from becoming too sour. If the milk is not chilled quickly enough the curds separate and the yogurt becomes watery. If the milk is kept too warm the bacteria are destroyed and the milk doesn't "thicken" into yogurt. There are several ways to make yogurt at home. Of course, it is possible to buy an electric yogurt maker, but there are simple methods of making good yogurt using those utensils you already have on hand.

HOMEMADE YOGURT 1

3 tablespoons commercial plain yogurt
2 tablespoons nonfat dry milk
2½ cups milk

Prepare jar by pouring boiling water into it and letting it stand for a few minutes before emptying. (Make sure you put a spoon into the jar or it might crack.) Mix dried milk and whole milk. Heat in a saucepan carefully until it almost reaches the boiling point. Set aside to cool. (Test with a clean finger— milk should feel just warm.) Mix in commercial yogurt starter and pour into prepared jar. Screw on lid and wrap jar in a piece of clean blanket and place in a plastic bucket. Put the bucket in a warm spot in the house. Allow to stand for about 6 hours. Unwrap and refrigerate. Reserve 3 tablespoons for the next batch.

HOMEMADE YOGURT 2

2 cups warm water
1½ cups nonfat dry milk (whole or
  skim or a mixture)
3 tablespoons commercial plain yogurt
1 cup evaporated milk
2½ cups warm water

Place the two cups of warm water, dry milk solids, and yogurt starter in a bowl and mix with an eggbeater. Then add the evaporated milk and 2½ cups warm water; mix well. Pour into a warmed 6-cup casserole or into jars. Stand in an electric fry pan on several layers of newspaper or on an asbestos mat. Set fry pan at 100°F. Allow to stand 6 hours, then refrigerate.

HOMEMADE YOGURT 3

½ cup nonfat dry milk
3 tablespoons commercial plain yogurt
3 cups warm water

Place all ingredients in a blender; blend well. Pour into prepared screw-top jars and place in electric yogurt maker, or place jars in a baking dish, half filled with warm water, in an oven kept warm by the pilot light. Allow to stand 6 hours, or until set.

Yogurt can also be made using any of the above recipes and pouring the mixture into a vacuum bottle to set. When set, pour into jars and refrigerate.

IDEAS FOR SERVING YOGURT

YOGURT APPLE
5 months

3 tablespoons plain yogurt
2 tablespoons Applesauce
½ teaspoon honey (optional)

Place ingredients in a blender, blend well, or mix well with spoon. Yogurt may be poured into a bottle or fed to the baby on a spoon.

FRUIT YOGURT
5 months

Great for the whole family!

Mix yogurt with any fresh or cooked fruit in season. No need to add sugar! If the fruit is especially sour, add a little honey. Serve fruit yogurt for breakfast, lunch, or as a dessert.

CAROB YOGURT
8 months

Introduce carob (see page 22) carefully—just sprinkle over yogurt or milk at first.

2 tablespoons plain yogurt
1 teaspoon carob powder

Mix and serve.

YOGURT ICE STICKS
18 months

These make delicious alternatives to the expensive, unhealthy, bought variety! Mix yogurt with any fruit in season and pour into ice cube trays. Partially freeze. Add sticks. Freeze till firm.

FRUIT YOGURT FROZEN DELIGHT
18 months

8 oz. dried apricots
2 teaspoons unflavored gelatin
2 tablespoons hot water
1 cup plain yogurt
2 egg whites
¼ cup granulated sugar

Soak apricots overnight in water to cover. Simmer gently until tender; drain. Sprinkle gelatine into the hot water, stir until dissolved; pour into container of blender. Add the cooked apricots; blend until smooth. Add yogurt and blend. Pour into a large, shallow container suitable for putting into the freezer. Freeze until ice has begun to form around the edge of container; remove, and break up ice with a fork. Beat egg whites until peaks form, gradually beat in sugar, and beat until egg whites are stiff. Fold into yogurt-fruit mixture, pour into ice cube trays, and freeze until firm.

Instead of apricots you might like to try this dessert with 8 oz. of berries, e.g., strawberries, or 2 large ripe bananas, fresh pineapple, or whatever fruit is in season.

5
CEREALS

Introducing natural grains—the health-building alternatives to packaged, precooked cereals

From infancy to adulthood, grains have an important place in our diet, usually as bread and as a breakfast cereal. Sadly, instead of our grain being a fine, nutritious food, too often it is eaten in the form of bleached white bread or highly processed, overheated, nutritionless packaged cereal. Not only are the cereals packaged for children and adults at fault, but those precooked cereals packaged for babies may have the vital nutrients refined away and a high salt content added.

These cereals add up to low nutrition—a very poor way to start the day! Also, if you read cereal labels you will find that many popular cereals have a high sugar content, especially the sugar-coated, chocolate-flavored variety.

For your family's sake, discover the health-building, delicious natural grains—rice, oats, bran, wheat, corn. Dress them up for variety and fun, to look and taste better with some of the following suggestions:

1. Mix in fruit, fresh or cooked (puréed for the very young), including raisins and apricots for older children.
2. Sprinkle on generous quantities of wheat germ, either fresh or toasted.
3. Make faces on bowls of cereal with drizzled honey or yogurt, or use pieces of fruit for eyes, nose, etc.
4. Add nonfat dry milk for extra protein and flavor.

Of course, there will be mornings when packaged cereal will be all you can manage, but don't forget that it takes only seconds to pep it up with a sprinkle of wheat germ and a dash of brewer's yeast! (Brewer's yeast is available at health food stores and is just packed with B vitamins and iron.)

As stated elsewhere, I prefer fruit and yogurt as first solids, but if you decide or are advised to introduce cereals first, the recipes included here for young babies will be useful.

RICE

Grind several cups of raw brown rice (½ cup at a time) in a blender or food processor. Store the flour in a tightly covered container.

RICE CREAM
4 months

Pour slowly into the top of a double boiler (or use a heavy saucepan over low heat) ¼ cup Rice Flour (made as above) and 1 cup water. Cook until creamy, about 10 minutes, stirring constantly to prevent lumps.

Add a little extra formula or milk if a more liquid consistency is desired. This quantity is enough for 2 servings—store half in the refrigerator and warm up for next time.

RICE SMOOTHIE
6 months

This cereal can be served with honey, wheat germ, Yogurt, mashed banana, or a combination!

½ cup Rice Flour
2 cups milk

In a small saucepan, bring milk to just below boiling point. Add the Rice Flour, stirring constantly. Lower heat, cover saucepan, and simmer gently for 10 minutes.

RICE PUDDING
18 months

Yes, for breakfast! Make this a day ahead and serve cold.

2 cups cooked brown rice	*2 eggs, well beaten*
2 cups milk	*½ teaspoon vanilla extract*
½ cup nonfat dry milk	*¼ cup raisins*
¼ cup brown sugar or honey	*¼ cup golden raisins*
1½ teaspoons melted butter	*wheat germ*

Mix all ingredients together except wheat germ. Butter a 4-cup casserole dish, pour in rice pudding mixture, and sprinkle wheat germ over. Bake at 350°F for 20 minutes. Serve cold with extra milk and fresh fruit.

RICE MEDLEY
20 months

A simple, nutritious meal that can be served hot or cold, stores well, and can use up leftovers is a joy to any mother. Such is the basic rice medley, or rice salad.

Start with 1 cup of cooked, natural brown rice and add any combination of chopped meats and vegetables, cold hard-cooked eggs, cheese cubes, fresh or canned flaked fish, or grated apple. Simply adjust the combinations and textures to suit the age of the child. Rice medley can be simple enough to suit the fussiest eater, say, chopped eggs and tuna, or exotic enough to suit the most adventurous. You can cook and store rice in a covered container in the refrigerator, so it's possible to make a cold rice salad or hot rice medley in a very short time. To warm rice, place in a metal colander over boiling water and steam for a few minutes or mix with vegetable/meat combinations, add a little butter or milk, and stir over low heat till heated through.

OATS

Introduce oats gradually, as they may cause rashes in some children. Grind rolled oats in a blender; store in covered container. Ground oats cook faster and save time during morning "rush hour."

BASIC OATMEAL
5 months

½ cup rolled oats, unground
2½ cups boiling water

Pour oats slowly into boiling water. Cover and simmer 30 minutes. Add milk or formula for desired consistency.

BANANA OATMEAL
5 months

Instead of banana, try Applesauce or puréed pear.

½ cup ground oats
1 cup water, milk, or formula
½ ripe banana
½ cup milk or plain Yogurt

Mix ground oats and 1 cup of water, milk, or formula in a saucepan. Bring to a boil, then simmer for 4–5 minutes, stirring constantly. Remove from heat, cover, and let stand 5 minutes longer. Slice banana into a blender, add remaining milk or yogurt, and blend. When cooked cereal is ready, stir in banana-milk and mix.

CORN

HOT CORN CEREAL
8 months

¼ cup yellow cornmeal
¼ cup cold water
2 teaspoons wheat germ
¾ cup boiling water
¼ cup nonfat dry milk (optional)

Mix together cornmeal, cold water, and wheat germ. Bring ¾ cup water to a boil, add the cornmeal mixture and nonfat dry milk, if you are using it.

Stirring constantly, bring to a boil, and simmer for 2 minutes. Serve with honey, fresh puréed fruit, or for older children, add raisins or chopped dates.

CORNMEAL MUSH
8 months

½ cup water
¼ cup cornmeal

Bring water to a boil in a small saucepan, slowly stir in cornmeal, and cook until mushy—about 15 minutes.

WHEAT GERM

In the center of the wheat kernel is the embryo or germ of the wheat which contains most of the vitamins and minerals—it is this germ which is discarded in the milling process of refined wheat flour. This vitamin- and mineral-rich germ can be bought at health food stores and some supermarkets. Learn to use it, not only for babies and children but for all the family. It's great as a cereal raw or toasted, with milk and fruit, sprinkled on vegetables, in casseroles and stews; substitute it in recipes where you would normally use bread crumbs, e.g., meat loaf, hamburgers, breaded fish, breaded chicken—the list is endless.

Wheat germ should be refrigerated to prevent rancidity.

Don't give wheat germ to babies under 6 months! After that age, seek the advice of your doctor before introducing it, as a certain proportion of the population is allergic to gluten (a cereal protein).

When you do introduce it, start gradually by sprinkling it on other cereals until the baby can eat it on its own as a cereal with milk. Some children don't like the wheat germ raw, so toast some to make it more palatable; although less nutritious than raw wheat germ this is preferable to packaged cereals!

TOASTED WHEAT GERM
Over 6 months

½ cup honey
4 cups wheat germ

Warm the honey a little, add to wheat germ and mix thoroughly; spread mixture on a well-greased cookie sheet. Bake at 300°F for 10 minutes in bottom third of oven. Store in airtight containers in refrigerator.

WHEAT GERM-YOGURT BREAKFAST
6 months

This is a very quick, nutritious breakfast the whole family will enjoy. Vary quantities to suit various tastes.

1 tablespoon wheat germ
2 tablespoons plain Yogurt
1 teaspoon honey

1 tablespoon Puréed Raw Apple or
mashed banana for baby, or any
fruit for the family

Mix all ingredients together and serve.

COTTAGE CHEESE PANCAKES
Over 2 years

3 eggs
1 cup cottage cheese
1½ tablespoons melted butter

1½ tablespoons whole wheat flour
1½ teaspoons wheat germ

With a mixer, or in a blender, beat eggs, add cottage cheese, and mix till fairly smooth. Add butter, flour, and wheat germ. Pour small quantity into a lightly greased frying pan; cook as for pancakes. Serve with Applesauce or apricot purée.

36

CEREAL BALLS
Over 2 years

1 cup granola
2 tablespoons wheat germ
2 teaspoons chopped egg yolk
1 tablespoon honey

1 tablespoon Peanut Butter (optional)
¼ cup chopped raisins
1½ teaspoons brewer's yeast
milk—as much as needed

Grind cereal in blender, add remaining ingredients except milk, and blend. Add as much milk as needed to bind mixture and enable you to roll it into balls. Refrigerate in covered container. For variety, try rolling some of the balls in freshly shredded coconut.

HOMEMADE BREAD

Good toasted and served in fingers for those over 12 months.

BREAKFAST BANANA NUT BREAD

¼ cup butter or margarine
½ cup brown sugar
1 egg, beaten
1 cup bran cereal or rolled oats
4–5 mashed ripe bananas
1 teaspoon vanilla extract
1½ cups whole wheat flour
2 teaspoons baking powder
½ teaspoon baking soda
½ teaspoon salt
½ cup chopped nuts (see Note below)

Cream shortening and sugar, add egg, mix well. Add cereal, bananas, and vanilla; stir. Combine remaining ingredients in a bowl and add to first mixture, stirring only long enough to moisten flour. Grease a loaf pan and sprinkle with flour (or use cooking spray); pour in mixture. Bake at 350°F for about 1 hour.

Note: If this bread will be eaten by your under-fours, make sure you grind the nuts in a blender before adding to mixture.

HIGH-PROTEIN CORNBREAD

1 cup cornmeal
⅓ cup soy flour (see Note below)
¼ cup whole wheat flour
2 teaspoons baking soda
½ teaspoon salt
1 egg
1 cup liquid milk with ¼ cup nonfat
  dry milk added
3 tablespoons honey

Mix dry ingredients together. Beat liquid ingredients together and add to the dry, beating until smooth. Pour into greased loaf pan and bake about 30 minutes at 375°F.

Delicious hot from the oven for the older members of the family, great toasted for small children and babies over 10 months.

Note: If not available in your supermarket, try a Chinese or Japanese food store or health food store.

RUSKS

Using only whole wheat bread, cut slices about 1 inch thick. Cut off crusts, then cut into strips about ½ inch wide. Bake in a slow oven for about 1 hour, or until they are dry and crisp. Cool and keep in an airtight container. These will cheer a miserable teething baby.

6
EXPLORING VEGETABLES

Vegetables "straight" and in delicious combinations for the baby and the whole family

Too often the serving of tasteless, waterlogged, uninteresting vegetables leads to babies and older children developing the "Yuk, vegetables" habit! Instead of relishing the abundant variety of taste and texture, children come to regard vegetable eating as an unpleasant chore, a punishment, and it becomes a bind for both parent and child. This sad situation can be avoided with a little care and imagination, and exploring vegetables with their wealth of health- and vitality-giving vitamins and minerals can be a delight to both cook and children.

There are a few important points to keep in mind when buying and preparing vegetables. Remember that you get poor value for your money if you try to economize with wilted, bruised, "old" vegetables. These have lost a considerable percentage of their valuable vitamin C, so always look for the freshest vegetables in season and buy and eat them as soon as possible. Avoid canned vegetables whenever possible; for flavor and nutrition, fresh vegetables really are the best value, but quick-freezing means that vitamin loss is minimized.

To ensure maximum flavor and vitamin retention when preparing the delicious fresh vegetables you have grown or bought, here are some very important don'ts:

Don't soak vegetables—a thorough wash under running water or a scrub with a vegetable brush is all that is needed.

Don't add baking soda or salt to vegetables—this kills valuable nutrients.

Don't, please, boil the life out of vegetables! Apart from spoiling the flavor, texture, and appearance, overcooking destroys vitamins.

Cook vegetables in a small amount of boiling water in a tightly covered saucepan until they are just tender for the baby, still slightly crisp for the older children. Keep any leftover cooking liquid for giving to baby in his bottle, for using to add to other baby foods, or for puréeing dry foods. Steaming is an ideal way to prepare vegetables. Steam them over boiling water for a few minutes for delicious flavor. Steamers are inexpensive little gadgets that fit into any size saucepan.

Don't peel vegetables like potatoes and squash before cooking. Cook with the skin on and then peel. Carrots need only to be scraped lightly, not peeled. Zucchini should be scraped for little children as sometimes the skin has a bitter flavor.

Do use lots of parsley and lemon juice to give vegetables a lift; both are rich in vitamin C. Grated cheese, egg yolk, chopped fresh herbs and yogurt all add variety and interest to vegetable cooking.

The following is a suggested order in which to introduce a baby to vegetables:

Carrots	Squash and zucchini
Sweet potato	Peas
Pumpkin	Spinach
Potato	Green beans

VEGETABLE PURÉE
4 months

To purée vegetables, simply steam or boil them in as little water as possible till tender, then blend them with the cooking liquid left over. Mashing thoroughly with a fork or pushing vegetables through a sieve or a mouli are alternatives.

Vegetable purées make marvelous "starters" for a variety of meals. Try some of the following combinations for babies from 6 months of age:

vegetable purée with cottage cheese
vegetable purée with plain Yogurt
vegetable purée with Unsweetened Custard
vegetable purée with egg yolk
vegetable purée with wheat germ
vegetable purée with brewer's yeast
vegetable purée with Scrambled Egg

Make purée into soup by adding extra milk, formula, vegetable cooking water, or stock—a great lunch idea when served with whole wheat toast and a fruit yogurt dessert.

It is a great time-saving idea to make large quantities of purée at once and freeze it using the ice-cube-tray method, for later use on busy days.

For the baby over 6 months, mix and match vegetable purées, or add a little fruit for variety. A little scraped apple or mashed banana does wonders for mashed potato!

SQUASH AND PUMPKIN

Two vegetables which make ideal "firsts" for a baby are squash and pumpkin. Both have a sweet, smooth texture baby will love and are easily digested. Any variety of squash is suitable, but the particularly delicious flavor of butternut squash makes it a favorite with babies and children. Butternut squash is an extremely versatile vegetable and can be prepared in many different ways for babies, older children, and the whole family.

BUTTERNUT SQUASH
4 months

Cut squash into chunks (don't peel) and steam until tender. Scrape the squash from the skin and mash or purée in a blender or food processor.

When preparing butternut squash for the whole family, bake one whole until tender. Simply remove enough for the baby and serve the remainder sprinkled with parsley to the family.

BUTTERNUT SQUASH SOUP
6 months

1 whole butternut squash
1 large potato
1 white onion, chopped (optional)
½–1 cup milk

Cut unpeeled squash and potato into segments. Cover, and boil with onion in a minimum of water, until cooked. Remove vegetables, peel, and place with remaining liquid into blender; blend till smooth. Add enough milk to make soup the consistency your baby likes.

For the family—season to taste; add a sprinkle of nutmeg, parsley, or chives.

For a dinner party—try soup with a dollop of sour cream and a generous sprinkling of nutmeg.

PUMPKIN PIE
6 months

1 cup cooked, mashed pumpkin
½ cup cottage cheese
1 tablespoon wheat germ

Butter a small ovenproof dish. Combine pumpkin and cheese; place in dish. Sprinkle wheat germ over. Bake in a moderate oven until the wheat germ is toasted.

CARROTS

CARROT CUSTARD
6 months

1 cup puréed carrot
1 cup Unsweetened Egg Custard
chopped parsley

Unsweetened Egg Custard

2 cups milk or formula
2 egg yolks

Beat milk and egg yolks together, heat gently, stirring constantly until custard coats a metal spoon. Remove from heat immediately; cool. Store in covered container in refrigerator.

Mix together carrot purée and custard; sprinkle with chopped parsley. Serve warm or cold.

CARROTS 'n' CHEESE
8 months

½ cup cottage cheese
½ cup finely grated carrot
chopped parsley

Combine all ingredients. Spread mixture onto whole wheat toast fingers or use as a sandwich filling for children over 15 months.

CARROT AND CHEESE BAKE
12 months

12 carrots, medium size
¼ cup butter
¼ cup whole wheat flour
2 cups milk

8 oz. grated cheese
½ cup wheat germ
½ cup whole wheat bread crumbs

Cook carrots till just tender. Slice. Melt butter in a pan, stir in flour, and cook for one minute. Gradually add milk, stirring continuously until sauce is thick and smooth. Place carrots and cheese in alternate layers in a buttered casserole dish, ending with a layer of carrots. Pour over sauce; sprinkle wheat germ and bread crumbs on top. Dot with butter. Bake for 20 minutes in a moderate oven.

POTATO

BAKED POTATO AND APPLE PIE
6 months

1 red apple
¾ cup cooked sweet potato
¼ cup milk, or for the breast-fed baby
  use cooking water or any leftover
  vegetable water
wheat germ

Peel and slice apple. Butter a small ovenproof dish; put in apple slices and sweet potato in alternate layers. Pour liquid over; sprinkle wheat germ over. Cover and bake for 30 minutes at 350°F.
  To serve, mash with a fork.

SWEET POTATO CUSTARD
6 months

¼ cup puréed sweet potato (carrots
  make a delicious alternative, so do
  winter squash or pumpkin)
1 egg yolk, beaten
¼ cup milk or formula

Blend together ingredients and pour into a buttered ovenproof dish or use individual custard cups.
  Place in a pan of water and bake at 375°F until set, about 30 minutes.

CHEESY SPINACH POTATO PIE
8 months

½ cup cooked spinach
1 cup cooked mashed potato
1 tablespoon grated cheese
wheat germ

Prepare spinach by washing thoroughly and removing the tough inner stalk. Shred, place in a saucepan with very little water and cook 5 minutes. When making this recipe for babies under 12 months, purée the spinach; for the older ones, simply chop finely.

Combine vegetables and cheese and place in a buttered ovenproof dish. Sprinkle with wheat germ and bake for 15 minutes in a moderate oven.

POTATO SOUFFLÉ
12 months

¾ cup cooked mashed potato
2 tablespoons grated cheese (optional—
  may be indigestible)
½ cup milk, warm

2 eggs, separated
1½ teaspoons melted butter
salt (not for those under 18 months)

Mix potato, cheese, milk and a sprinkle of salt; add beaten egg yolks and melted butter. Mix stiffly beaten egg whites into mixture as lightly as possible. Place in buttered ovenproof dish and sprinkle over cheese. Bake in moderate oven until brown.

EGG IN THE NEST
12 months

For older babies and children, vary the "nest" by using cooked chopped spinach and grating a little cheese over the egg before baking.

2 tablespoons cooked sweet potato,
  mashed

1 egg
1 teaspoon butter

Butter a small ramekin, make a "nest" in it with the potato and break an egg into it. Place a teaspoon of butter on top of the egg and bake in a moderate oven for 15 minutes or until egg is set.

POTATO PANCAKES
18 months

These pancakes are delicious served with unsweetened Applesauce.

3 large potatoes
1 egg, well beaten
1 tablespoon whole wheat flour
chopped parsley
a little salt

Peel and grate potatoes; mix with beaten egg. Add flour, parsley and salt; mix well. Heat oil in a frying pan and pour in potato mixture, a tablespoon at a time. Cook until golden. Drain well.

PARSNIPS

Parsnips are valuable vegetables too often used only in soups and stews. Babies from the age of 6 months love parsnips cooked till tender and mashed thoroughly with a little butter and chopped parsley. As with all new foods, they should be introduced ½ teaspoonful first, to check baby's reactions.

Serve them often to older children, too, as a change from potatoes.

ZUCCHINI

ZUCCHINI SLURP
6 months

Try adding puréed carrot to zucchini slurp for a new taste.

3 medium-sized zucchini
2 tablespoons plain Yogurt
chopped parsley

Wash and scrape zucchini; steam until tender. Mash well, then fold in yogurt and chopped parsley.

ZUCCHINI PIE
18 months

1 lb. zucchini, peeled
½ onion, sliced (optional)
4 eggs
1 cup grated cheese

½ teaspoon each of dried oregano and
basil (for children over 2 years)
salt and pepper

Steam zucchini and onion until tender. Beat eggs; add cheese. Mash zucchini and onion and add to eggs and cheese. Add herbs and salt and pepper. Pour into a greased baking dish, cover and bake at 325°F until set, about 30–40 minutes.

This pie can be varied by adding different herbs or by adding leftover meats like chicken or lamb. For a delicious special dish add fresh steamed shrimp and serve with a crisp salad.

PEAS

Babies usually love peas, so serve them often. Simply cook till tender and purée for the younger baby. For variety mix in Applesauce or cottage cheese. Peas make an excellent finger food for the older baby (12–14 months). Simply place cooked peas directly onto baby's high-chair tray and watch him enjoy himself! A good way to combine good nutrition with lots of fun and co-ordination development.

CHEESY PEAS
7 months

½ cup cooked peas
1 tablespoon grated cheese

Combine and blend. For the older baby, simply mash with a fork.

SPINACH

SPINACH SOUFFLÉ
18 months

2 tablespoons butter
3 tablespoons whole wheat flour
1/2 cup milk
1/2 cup grated cheese
salt and pepper

2 eggs, separated
8 oz. fresh spinach, shredded or finely
    chopped
1/2 teaspoon nutmeg (optional)

Melt butter, add flour, and cook gently for one minute. Add milk gradually, stirring continuously until sauce thickens. Add cheese, salt and pepper; cook until cheese melts. Beat egg yolks thoroughly and add gradually to sauce. Cool. Add spinach. Beat egg whites until stiff, then fold into spinach mixture. Pour into greased soufflé dish, sprinkle with nutmeg, and bake in a slow oven for 1 hour, or until soufflé is well risen and golden brown.

SPINACH ROLL-UPS
2 years

This makes a delicious family meal, a great and cheap alternative to meat.

1 lb. spinach
1/2 cup brown rice, cooked
1/2 cup cottage cheese
1/2 cup chopped walnuts (grind these in
    a blender if serving to children
    under 4)

2 tablespoons raisins
1 small white onion, chopped
    (optional)
1 cup tomato juice
1/2 cup grated cheese

Wash spinach carefully; remove stems. Blanch spinach leaves in boiling water for 1 minute.

Combine rice, cottage cheese, walnuts, raisins, and onion. Add a little salt and pepper.

Place a tablespoon of rice mixture on each spinach leaf and roll up, being careful to completely enclose filling. Place spinach rolls in a buttered casserole dish. Pour over tomato juice and sprinkle with grated cheese. Bake in a moderate oven for 15–20 minutes.

CABBAGE

MILKY CABBAGE
18 months

Cabbage cooked this way has a mild flavor children like, and the likelihood of "gas" is reduced.

1 small cabbage
1 cup milk

Shred cabbage; add milk. Cook in tightly covered saucepan until cabbage is tender but not overcooked. For variety, try adding a little grated cheese before serving.

OTHER VEGETABLES

VEGETABLE HOT POT
18 months

2 carrots
3 potatoes
2 turnips
3 onions (optional)
chopped parsley
½ bunch celery
1 cup pea beans
3 cups Chicken Stock
salt and pepper
1 cup grated cheese

Prepare beans by soaking in water to cover overnight, then boiling them until tender, about 1½–2 hours.

Prepare vegetables, slice and place in layers with parsley in a flameproof saucepan with stock. Bring to a boil, lower heat and gently simmer until vegetables are tender, about 40 minutes. Sprinkle with grated cheese and place in oven or under broiler until cheese melts.

VEGETABLE BAKE
12 months

A good lunch idea for preschoolers.

2 potatoes	1 ½ teaspoons whole wheat flour
2 or 3 carrots	2 cups milk
1 lb. pumpkin	1 cup grated cheese
1 cup green beans	½ cup wheat germ
parsley	1 ½ teaspoons butter

Cook all vegetables separately till tender; place in layers with parsley in buttered casserole dish. Melt butter in saucepan, remove from heat, stir in flour, and cook gently 1 minute. Gradually stir in milk and grated cheese until sauce thickens. Pour cheese sauce over vegetables; cover top with wheat germ. Dot with butter and bake, uncovered, until wheat germ is brown.

You can use any combination of vegetables in Vegetable Bake—try adding fresh, chopped tomatoes, cooked celery or green peas.

TOMATO SAUCE
12 months

Many children love tomato sauce splashed over everything, so make your own, free from artificial coloring and preservatives. I find it delicious served with vegetables and eggs as well as meat dishes.

1 lb. very ripe, peeled tomatoes	1 tablespoon parsley
1 large chopped onion (optional)	pinch dried thyme or sprig of fresh
5 stalks celery, chopped and with	3 tablespoons oil or margarine
"strings" removed	2 tablespoons whole wheat flour
½ teaspoon salt	1 teaspoon honey

Blend first six ingredients well in a blender. (If not using a blender, mash thoroughly, sieve tomatoes to remove seeds, and extend cooking time about 10 minutes.)

Heat oil or margarine; blend in flour. Stir in tomato sauce with honey very gradually, simmer and stir until mixture thickens. Place in screw-top jar and store in refrigerator.

PASTA WITH TOMATO SAUCE

Pasta makes a quick weekend meal for tired moms who want to serve a satisfying but easily prepared family meal. But please don't reach for cans of precooked spaghetti! Making your own pasta is fun but timeconsuming—far easier to buy whole-grain pasta now available at most supermarkets. Cook it according to instructions on the package and serve with one of the following toppings:

Hot Homemade Tomato Sauce and a generous grating of cheese, or crisp crumbled bacon, or both!

Cooked ground beef in tomato sauce.

Tomato sauce and cooked green beans.

RABBIT FOOD

Older children going through a stage of saying "no" to anything looking like a cooked vegetable will often eat and enjoy crisp, raw vegetables, with or without a tasty dip. Arrange on a plate a variety of raw vegetables, e.g., cauliflower, carrots, mushrooms, celery, tomatoes, lettuce, green and red peppers, cucumber, peas in the pod, green beans, pieces of cabbage.

A delicious dip for raw vegetables can be made by combining equal parts of homemade Tomato Sauce with plain yogurt. Cream cheese beaten with homemade Tomato Sauce is another great dip.

Grated carrots mixed with raisins and blended with a little honey and lemon juice and piled onto lettuce leaves will often appeal to tired summer appetites.

Keep a ready supply of washed, prepared vegetable sticks in the crisper of your refrigerator for between-meal snacks or to keep children happy in that difficult half hour before dinner!

DRIED BEANS AND LENTILS

Dried beans and lentils are not suitable for babies under 12 months as they are too difficult to digest, but for older babies and children, beans and lentils provide an excellent source of protein, especially soybeans, which are as high in protein as meat. Beans and lentils are good value as they are inexpensive, store well and are easy to prepare. They make great lunch ideas for hungry toddlers—just mash and serve.

BASIC BEAN RECIPE

1 lb. dried pea or navy beans
4 cups water, or leftover vegetable water
sprig parsley
stalk celery (optional)
bay leaf
1 onion, chopped (optional)

Soak beans overnight. Add vegetables, bring to a boil, then cover and simmer until tender, about 2 hours. Soybeans may take longer to cook.

BEANS IN TOMATO SAUCE
12 months

1 lb. dried beans
1 cup homemade Tomato Sauce

Cook beans according to directions above. When tender, drain thoroughly and mix with tomato sauce. For variety, mix grated cheese through warm bean mixture.

BAKED SOYBEANS
15 months

1 lb. soybeans (see Note below)
1 cup chopped onion (optional)
½ cup oil
1 tablespoon honey
2 cups fresh homemade Tomato Sauce
    or tomato purée
salt

Soak beans overnight. Bring to a boil; simmer till tender. In an ovenproof pan sauté onion in oil until golden, add beans and remaining cooking water, honey, tomato sauce and a little salt. Bake uncovered in a moderate oven for 20 minutes.
Note: This dish can be made with pea or navy beans if preferred.

LENTILS AND TOMATOES
12 months

1 lb. lentils
2½ cups water
2 cups homemade Tomato Sauce

Soak lentils for 1 hour in water. Boil in same water until soft, about 30 minutes. When cooked, stir through tomato sauce.

SAVORY LENTILS
15 months

1 lb. lentils
2½ cups water
½ cup chopped onion (optional)
1 cup chopped, peeled tomatoes
2 tablespoons chopped parsley

Soak lentils for 1 hour. Boil until soft in the same water. Sauté onion until golden in a little oil or margarine, stir in tomatoes and parsley and cook until "mushy." Mix into cooked lentils. Serve with boiled brown rice for a nourishing winter lunch for preschoolers.

7
AND NOW—
EGGS FOR ALL

The versatile, nutritious egg—the ultimate time-saver for health conscious but busy mothers

Eggs have been called the "wonder food," and with good reason. They are tiny storehouses of protein, minerals, vitamins, and, very importantly, iron. Eggs are a marvelous food for babies and children—on their own or mixed with other foods. They are nutritious, easily digested, and quickly and simply prepared.

Eggs can be prepared in so many ways: as well as the simple soft- or hard-cooked, poached or scrambled eggs, they can be dressed up for fun and variety in salads, in cheese or savory sauces, mashed with fruits and vegetables, or cooked in puddings and desserts. Blended with milk or fruit juice, they make quick pick-me-ups for tired mothers, harried fathers, sick or busy children. And eggs are great value for the money—compare the cost with the nutrition received and you will realize that eggs are economical, indeed.

There need be no waste either, even the eggshell has a valuable use—*if you have a blender*. Save the shells from eggs you have hard-cooked and blend them with babies' milk or formula, or add shells blended with juice or yogurt to main meals for toddlers and older children. The eggshell is an extremely valuable and cheap source of extra calcium. It can be an important source of added calcium for pregnant and nursing mothers; just throw an eggshell into the blender with milk and fruit and there you have it—vitality plus!

When buying eggs, shop around for the freshest farm eggs—try fruit and vegetable markets as well as supermarkets.

Be guided by your doctor as to the best time to begin introducing eggs into your baby's diet. From six months on is the usual suggested time because it is at this age that the iron stored from birth needs to be supplemented, and egg yolk is a rich source of iron.

When introducing eggs to young babies it is recommended that only well-cooked egg *yolks* be tried; often raw or undercooked egg whites can produce allergic reactions. So do take care; start with ¼ teaspoon of egg yolk and gradually go on from there. In no time baby will be feeding himself Humpty Dumpties or demanding Banana Egg Milk!

EGG YOLK
6 months

As mentioned above, for the very young, introduce the hard-cooked yolk of egg first, in very small quantities. If no allergic reaction occurs, gradually increase the amount of egg yolk until a whole yolk is being taken. It is a good idea to mix the egg yolk with something very soft and slippery—mashed banana is fine! Add a little hard-cooked egg yolk to puréed vegetables, or simply mash it with milk, yogurt or water.

Once your baby is really enjoying his whole egg yolk, you can begin gradually to introduce the cooked egg white. As it is mostly to the white part of the egg that some children have allergic reactions, take care and introduce it slowly, making sure it is thoroughly cooked.

HARD-COOKED EGG
8–9 months

Place whole egg in a small saucepan, cover with cold water, bring water to a boil, lower heat, and simmer egg for 3½ minutes. This should produce an egg with a completely set white and firm yet moist yolk.

RED EGG
8–9 months

A delicious way of serving a hard-cooked egg is to scoop out the cooked egg into a bowl and add a small, very ripe tomato which has been peeled. Mash egg and tomato together thoroughly.

POACHED EGG
8–9 months

Bring water to a boil in a small frying pan. Gently break an egg into the water and simmer until set, about 2–3 minutes. Remove the egg with a slotted spatula, and mash.

EGG FLIP
12 months

Eggs are a boon to mothers whose children won't eat—egg yolk, raw, added to a baby bottle of milk with a teaspoon of honey will often be relished when a cooked egg is refused. Use this to make a meal-in-a-bottle for sick, tired or just plain cranky children.

SCRAMBLED EGG
12 months

1 egg
1 tablespoon milk
1 teaspoon butter or margarine

Beat egg and milk together in a small bowl or cup. Melt butter in a saucepan, pour in egg mixture and stir until egg is set, light and fluffy.

Most children love scrambled egg, and it can be used as the base for many delicious meals. To scrambled eggs, try adding the following, either separately or in combinations:
1 tablespoon cottage cheese
1 tablespoon grated cheddar cheese
1½ teaspoons chopped parsley
sprinkle of wheat germ
leftover cooked vegetables
grated apple
drained canned corn (for older children)
crisp bacon pieces
mashed peeled tomato
1 tablespoon nonfat dry milk for added protein

FLUFFY CHEESE OMELETTE
12 months

1½ teaspoons grated cheese
1 teaspoon water
1 egg, separated
butter

Mix cheese, water and egg yolk. Whip egg white until stiff; fold into egg-yolk mixture. Melt butter in a pan, pour in egg-cheese mixture and allow to brown underneath. When bottom is browned, place under broiler for a few seconds to set top.

EGG CUSTARD
12 months

1 cup milk
1 egg
1 teaspoon honey
few drops vanilla extract, or sprinkle
  of cinnamon (optional)

Whisk all ingredients together. Stir over very low heat until custard coats a metal spoon. Remove from heat quickly to prevent custard from curdling. If it does curdle, you can save it by pouring it into a blender and blending until smooth again.

If you are making a savory custard, leave out the honey and vanilla or cinnamon and add 2 tablespoons puréed vegetables.

BANANA EGG MILK
12 months

This meal-in-a-bottle is very handy when you arrive home too late to prepare a meal for the baby or when he has had a very busy morning and is too tired to eat lunch.

1 cup milk
1 egg yolk (the white can be added for
  older children)
1 very ripe banana
1 teaspoon wheat germ
dash of brewer's yeast
1 teaspoon honey

Blend all ingredients in a blender until light and frothy. Strain into bottle or cup.

VEGETABLE PANCAKE
12 months

A good way to use up leftover vegetables is to mash them with a beaten egg, then lightly cook in melted butter like a pancake.

FRIED EGG
15 months

1 egg
1 teaspoon butter or margarine or
   vegetable cooking spray

Never fry eggs in fat for babies and children as this makes them too indigestible. Simply melt butter in a pan and gently fry egg until set. Don't cook over too high heat as this makes the egg white tough.

Sprinkle grated cheese or parsley over the egg while it is cooking for a taste change.

BULL'S EYE
15 months

1 slice whole wheat or mixed-grain
   bread
butter or margarine
1 egg

Use a round biscuit cutter or a small glass and cut out a round in the center of the bread. Spread butter or margarine on both sides and place slice in frying pan. Break egg carefully into hole in center and cook until egg is set.

CHEESE SOUFFLÉ
2 years

Although this soufflé takes a little time to prepare, it is well worth the trouble. Children love it, and it is especially good served cold the next day.

4 1/2 tablespoons butter
4 1/2 tablespoons whole wheat flour
2 cups milk
6 eggs, separated
2 cups grated cheese
1/2 teaspoon salt

Preheat oven to 300°F. Melt butter in a saucepan, add flour and stir well. Gradually add milk and stir continuously until mixture thickens. Add well beaten egg yolks. Add cheese and salt, stir, and let thicken over low heat. Beat egg whites until stiff; add to cheese mixture, stirring well. Pour into well buttered, straight-sided casserole or soufflé dish. Bake at 300°F for about 1 hour. When cooked, the top is a golden brown.

HUMPTY DUMPTIES
2 years

These are known to grown-ups as Scotch Eggs.

4 tablespoons ground beef or sausage
  meat
chopped parsley
3 hard-cooked eggs, shelled
2 tablespoons whole wheat flour
1 egg, beaten
4 tablespoons wheat germ
oil for frying

Mix together meat and parsley. Cover the hard-cooked eggs carefully with the meat, keeping them in an egg shape. Dip covered eggs into flour, brush well with beaten egg and cover well with wheat germ. Fry for 5 minutes in heated oil, then drain thoroughly on paper towels. To serve, cut in halves lengthwise, or add whole cold Humpty Dumpties to packed lunches and picnics.

8
FOR ADVANCED BEGINNERS— MEAT AND FISH

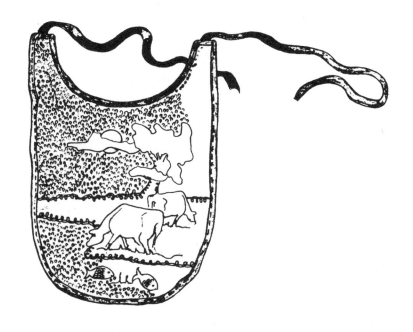

Meat and fish are usually introduced to babies some time after they have come to know and enjoy the various tastes and textures of fruits, yogurt, cereals, vegetables and egg yolk. There is no need at all to hurry a baby into eating meat and fish if he is already having a diet rich in protein and iron—be guided by your doctor.

I have found it best to begin by introducing the white meats; some poached chicken breast puréed in chicken stock, milk or yogurt until light and fluffy, or steamed fish puréed with milk, formula, or vegetable water till smooth. Next are variety meats, like liver, which are easier to digest than other red meats and which are packed with protein and iron—tremendous value for the money, too, as they are relatively cheap and there is no waste. Brains make ideal first meat meals for babies—a smooth texture and bland taste make them great favorites.

After the white meats, liver and brains, the red meats—veal, beef, and lamb—can be introduced. By this stage most meat prepared for the whole family should be suitable for the baby. Simply purée or finely chop or grind slices of roast meats or chops and steak and mix with beef stock or vegetable water. Babies don't like strong seasonings or too many herbs, so spicy meats such as curries will have to wait!

I haven't included pork or ham in the following recipes for babies and children, as these are the most indigestible of meats, often very greasy and unsuitable for young children.

CHICKEN

As well as being a family favorite, chicken is loved by babies and toddlers, too. They love its smooth texture and mild flavor. Chicken is easy to prepare and cooks quickly, which is a great help to busy mothers. Simply remove membranes and skin and it is ready to cook.

Chicken blends well with a variety of vegetables or it can be served as a simple purée with chicken stock or in hand-held, munching-size pieces for older babies and children.

CHICKEN STOCK

1 large chicken	*2 stalks celery, chopped*
4 cups water	*celery leaves*
2 onions, chopped (see Note below)	*2 carrots, diced*
parsley	*2 teaspoons salt (see Note below)*

Remove skin from chicken; cut meat into sections. Place chicken, vegetables, and water in a large saucepan, bring to a boil and gently simmer for 1½ hours. Chill. Skim fat from stock, then strain stock through a fine sieve. Store half in the refrigerator and freeze the remainder in ice cube trays.

Basic chicken stock can be used to purée chicken meat, or veal. Add it to leftover vegetables and purée to make nourishing winter soups. When reheating stock, add egg noodles to make your own chicken noodle soup, or cook natural brown rice in it and add vegetables and cooked chicken pieces for a hearty soup.

Note: Leave out the onion and salt if stock is to be used for very young babies.

CHICKEN PURÉE
6 months

1 chicken breast
1 cup Chicken Stock or water
sprig parsley

Remove skin from chicken and discard. Simmer chicken gently until cooked in a tightly covered saucepan with stock or water and parsley.

Remove chicken and cut away the meat from the bone. Place meat in blender and add enough of the cooking liquid to blend into a light and fluffy mixture.

Chicken purée can be made for the baby by reserving a few slices from the family roast or broiled chicken and puréeing it with one or two of your frozen chicken stock cubes. If you haven't any stock, milk, formula, water, apple juice and even yogurt make delicious chicken purée. If you are using meat from the family roast, take care to choose skinless, less fatty pieces.

APPLE CHICKEN
7 months

1 chicken breast, skinned and boned
1 red apple, peeled, cored and sliced
½ cup apple juice

Simmer chicken and sliced apple gently in apple juice until tender. Purée chicken, apple and cooking liquid in a blender until smooth for the tinies; for older babies and children, just mash with a fork. Apple Chicken is particularly delicious served with natural brown rice and peas.

CHICKEN STEW
8 months

1 chicken breast
1 cup Chicken Stock
1 potato, diced
1 carrot, diced

1 stalk celery, chopped
1 tomato, peeled
sprig parsley

Remove and discard skin and bones from chicken. Place all ingredients in a tightly covered saucepan and simmer gently for 30 minutes. For young babies, purée meat and vegetables with sufficient cooking liquid to make a smooth-textured mixture. For older babies and children, serve meat and vegetables separately, well mashed with a little stock poured over.

This stew freezes well, so it's a good idea to make double or triple quantities and freeze in small containers or use the ice cube tray method.

ORANGE CHICKEN
12 months

2 chicken legs and thighs, skin
   removed
pinch salt
chopped parsley

2 tablespoons melted butter
½ cup orange juice

Bone chicken and place in a small, buttered baking dish. Sprinkle with salt and parsley. Mix melted butter with orange juice, and pour over chicken. Bake for 30–40 minutes in a moderate oven, turning occasionally and basting with juice.

MUNCHING CHICKEN
12 months

4 chicken thighs
1 beaten egg
½–1 cup wheat germ or whole wheat
  bread crumbs
butter or margarine

Remove and discard skin from chicken thighs. Dip chicken into egg and wheat germ. Place chicken on a greased baking sheet or aluminum foil, dot with a little butter or margarine and bake in 350°F oven until cooked, about 30 minutes. Allow to cool, then hand to hungry babies and children! These make a great finger food for toddlers learning to feed themselves, and munching the bone is better than a rusk for teethers!

CHICKEN QUICHE
4–5 years

Delicious served cold in wedges for lunch.

Pie Shell
2 cups self-rising wheat flour
2½ teaspoons baking powder
¼ cup wheat germ

pinch salt
2 tablespoons butter
iced water

Sift flour, baking powder, wheat germ, and salt. Gently rub in butter until mixture resembles bread crumbs. Use enough iced water to make into a stiff dough. Chill dough in refrigerator for 30 minutes before rolling out and lining a 9-inch pie plate.

Filling
½ cup cooked, diced chicken
1½ cups grated cheddar cheese (mild)
3 eggs, lightly beaten

1½ cups milk
pinch salt
dash pepper

Place chicken and cheese in pie shell. Combine eggs, milk, salt and pepper, and pour over chicken and cheese. Bake at 375°F for 30–35 minutes, or until a knife inserted comes out clean. Allow to stand 10 minutes before serving.

FISH

Fish is great for babies and children because it is easy to chew and digest, has a delicate flavor, and is low in fat content. Also, fish is particularly nutritious, with vitamins and essential minerals like iodine, phosphorus, and magnesium.

Buy only really fresh fish: if it smells "fishy," it is stale! Make sure the eyes are bright and the flesh firm. Ask the fish dealer to fillet fish for you, as the fillets are less likely to have any bones. Boneless cod fillets are the best to buy for babies and young children; they are fleshy, with rarely any bones to worry about and with a bland, delicate flavor.

A good alternative to fresh fish is canned tuna or salmon, well drained. Don't give these to very young babies as they can often have a high salt content. However, low-sodium, water-packed tuna *is* available. Also, tuna can be rinsed to reduce salt content.

Be careful not to overcook fish. It is cooked when the flesh flakes with a fork but is still firm. Overcooked fish becomes tough and tasteless.

When you have cooked the fish for the baby or the older children, check and recheck for bones. Rubbing the fish through your fingers several times will allow you to feel any bones.

Although not cheap to buy, fresh fish is good value because it doesn't have any waste, so include it regularly in your family's meals.

POACHED FISH
7 months

1 cod fillet
½ cup milk, formula or vegetable
  cooking water
1 teaspoon butter

Place milk, fish and butter in saucepan, cover and simmer very gently until fish is cooked, about 10 minutes, or until fish flakes easily with a fork. For baby, blend fish and milk together, checking carefully with your fingers for bones before serving. For older babies, simply flake fish and serve with a little of the milk, checking for bones in the same way.

STEAMED FISH
7 months

1 cod fillet
½ cup milk or vegetable water
1 teaspoon butter
chopped parsley

Place all ingredients in a bowl above gently simmering water, or use a double boiler. Cover and steam until cooked. Check for bones with your fingers before serving.

FISH CUSTARD
8 months

1 cod fillet
1 cup unsweetened egg custard

Steam or poach fish until cooked. Check carefully for bones. Purée fish and custard together or for older babies, mash fish with a fork and stir into custard.

Unsweetened Egg Custard
2 cups milk or formula
2 egg yolks

Beat egg yolks and milk together, heat gently, stirring constantly until custard coats a metal spoon. Remove from heat immediately; cool. Store in a covered container in the refrigerator.

FISH CAKES
12 months

2 cups flaked fish (fresh or used canned tuna)
1 cup mashed potato
1 tablespoon chopped parsley
1 beaten egg
wheat germ

Combine all ingredients except the wheat germ. Shape mixture into balls and roll in wheat germ. Cook in a buttered ovenproof dish in a moderate oven for 10 minutes, or sauté in oil until brown for older babies and children.

FISH FANCY
15 months

1 large can salmon or tuna, drained	*¾ cup White Sauce*
juice of 1 lemon	*½ lb. tomatoes, peeled and sliced*
1 cup whole wheat bread crumbs	*1 cup grated mild cheddar cheese*

Mash fish, remove any bones. Place fish and lemon juice in a buttered ovenproof bowl, add half the bread crumbs, the white sauce and a layer of tomatoes. Cover with remaining bread crumbs, top with cheese and bake in a moderate oven for 20 minutes.

White Sauce
1 tablespoon butter or margarine
1 tablespoon whole wheat flour
1 cup milk

Melt butter over gentle heat, add flour and cook for 1 minute. Gradually pour in milk, stirring continuously until sauce thickens.

TUNA MORNAY
15 months

I find that everyone loves this nutritious, economical family meal.

1 large can tuna
1 cup cooked peas
2 hard-cooked eggs
1 cup White Sauce with 2 tablespoons
  of grated cheddar cheese mixed in
1 lb. potatoes, cooked and mashed
1 cup grated cheese

Drain tuna, flake with a fork and place in a buttered casserole. Add peas, halved hard-cooked eggs and white sauce. Cover with mashed potato; top with grated cheese. Bake in a moderate oven for 20 minutes.

You can add to the basic ingredients of this mornay: for variety, try cooked, diced carrots or zucchini, freshly chopped herbs, lemon juice, or a drop or two of tabasco sauce.

BAKED FISH
18 months

1 fish fillet (boneless cod is best)
little salt
few drops lemon juice
3 slices peeled tomato
1 teaspoon grated cheese
1 teaspoon wheat germ
chopped parsley
2 teaspoons butter

Place fish on a square of aluminum foil, large enough to enclose fish when folded. Sprinkle salt and lemon juice on fish, place tomato slices on top, then cheese and wheat germ mixed together. Top with parsley and pieces of butter. Fold over foil, sealing edges carefully. Bake in a moderate oven until cooked. Check fish carefully for bones before serving.

FISH FINGERS
18 months

1 lb. boneless fish
1 or 2 eggs, well beaten
wheat germ or cornmeal
vegetable oil

Cut fish into finger lengths or bite-sized pieces, if you prefer, dip into egg, then wheat germ or cornmeal. Refrigerate for an hour (this helps to keep the coating firmly on). Fry in a small quantity of vegetable oil, turning once, until cooked.

LIVER

Liver is one of the most nutritious foods you can give your babies and children. It is the richest natural source of iron and is high in protein, B vitamins and minerals. In fact, liver is more nutritious than muscle meats such as steak and chops and, importantly, is easier for babies to digest.

Probably because of unimaginative overcooking, liver is not usually popular family fare, so if *you* don't like it, try not to show that dislike when introducing it to your baby—he or she will be very quick to sense your feelings! Serve liver with a smile to your whole family and you will probably find they will love it.

Liver tastes surprisingly delicious when cooked with fruit. Babies love the combination of liver and orange or liver and apples. Even if liver hasn't been one of your favorite foods, you'll find it hard to resist the following dishes.

LIVER PÂTÉ 1
6 months

8 oz. liver (calf or chicken is suitable)
1 small tomato, peeled
½ carrot, scraped and sliced
½ potato, diced
¾ cup Beef Stock or water

Simmer liver and vegetables in stock gently for 8–10 minutes. Spoon vegetables and liver into blender and blend, adding cooking liquid as needed to get the right consistency. When thoroughly blended, serve.

LIVER PÂTÉ 2
12 months

This is a delicious pâté, very quick to make, and economical. It does double duty for both baby and family and for entertaining. When serving to guests, garnish pâté with slices of sautéed mushroom, chopped parsley, or grated egg yolk.

1 lb. chicken livers
2 white onions, sliced
4–6 tablespoons butter
2 hard-cooked eggs
salt and pepper to taste

Sauté onions in butter until golden. Remove and place in blender. Wash livers thoroughly and remove any dark spots and tissue. Dry and sauté gently until firm but still pink in the center, about 2 or 3 minutes. Place livers in blender with onions and hard-cooked eggs and salt and pepper and blend until smooth. Place in dish and chill.

LIVER STEW
7 months

8 oz. *lamb's liver, membrane removed,*
    chopped
½ cup *Beef Stock or water*
1 *carrot, scraped*
2 *stalks celery*
1 *potato, peeled and cubed*
½ *parsnip, peeled*

Cook vegetables for 5 minutes in stock, add chopped liver, and cook for another 5 minutes. For babies under 9 months, purée all ingredients together; for older babies and children, serve liver and vegetables separately, carefully mashed for those with limited chewing ability!

CHICKEN LIVER SOUP
7 months

2 *chicken livers*
1 *cup water*
1 *tablespoon rice or barley*
pinch of salt
½ cup milk

Simmer chicken livers, rice, salt and water until tender. Cool slightly and blend for one minute or until smooth. If not using a blender, sieve solids through a strainer back into the cooking liquid. Add ½ cup milk. Reheat.

LIVER AND APPLES 1
7 months

1 *lb. chicken livers*
2 *large Granny Smith apples, peeled*
    and sliced
1 *cup apple juice*

Place prepared livers, peeled and sliced apples and juice in a saucepan and simmer gently until apples and livers are cooked through. For babies under 9 months, mash thoroughly or purée in a blender.

LIVER AND APPLES 2
9 months

1 lb. chicken livers	*4 tablespoons butter or oil*
2 large red apples	*½ cup apple juice*

Prepare livers; peel and slice apples. Sauté together in butter or oil until partly cooked, then add apple juice and cook until liver and apples are tender.

LIVER AND BACON CASSEROLE
15 months

1 lamb's liver	*2 onions, sliced*
2 tablespoons whole wheat flour	*1 carrot, diced*
2 slices lean bacon	*parsley*
1 lb. tomatoes (use canned if fresh are not available), sliced	*1 cup Beef Stock or water*

Soak liver in cold water for 10 minutes—it makes it easier to remove the membrane. Dry and slice liver thinly, then roll in flour. Cut bacon into bite-sized pieces and arrange liver and bacon in layers with tomato, onion, carrot, and parsley in a casserole. Add stock. Cover and bake at 300°F for 1 hour.

LIVER IN WHEAT GERM
10 months

1 lb. calf's liver, washed and with membrane removed	*1 beaten egg*
whole wheat flour	*wheat germ*
	oil

Slice liver thinly into "fingers" for those under 18 months. Dip liver into flour, egg and wheat germ, then gently fry in oil until cooked through.

LIVER FINGERS
10 months

Liver fingers make ideal finger food, easy for small hands to hold and have a soft, easy-to-chew texture. Calf's or lamb's liver is best for this recipe. Buy a whole liver, remove membrane, and cut into fingers. Freeze individually and you have a ready supply of quick dinners and nutritious snacks on hand. There is no need to thaw fingers, just sauté in butter until firm but pinkish inside.

LIVER AND ORANGE
12 months

1 large orange
2 tablespoons wheat germ
1 lb. calf's liver

4 tablespoons butter or oil
salt and pepper to taste (for older
    children only)

Finely grate orange rind and mix with wheat germ, salt and pepper. Trim liver and cut into thin slices or fingers. Coat with seasoned wheat germ. Heat butter or oil in a heavy pan and sauté liver until cooked through; remove to a serving plate and keep warm. Squeeze juice from the orange, add to pan, and stir over heat. Spoon pan juice over liver and serve with mashed potato.

BRAINS

Brains are a simple and economical meal, and when they are prepared with a creamy sauce, I have found that babies and children really enjoy them.

LAMBS' BRAINS
6 months

2 sets lambs' brains (calves' can be
    used)

½ cup milk, formula, or stock

Soak brains in cold water for several hours. Remove any dark spots, skin and membranes. Place in a saucepan, cover with water and simmer for 10 minutes. Remove brains and blend with milk, formula or stock until smooth.

BRAINS IN CREAM SAUCE
9 months

2 sets brains (lamb or calf)
1½ teaspoons butter

1½ teaspoons whole wheat flour
1 cup milk or formula

Soak brains for several hours in cold water, then remove dark spots, skin, and membranes. Simmer in water to cover for 10 minutes. Make cream sauce by melting butter in a saucepan, stirring in flour, and gradually adding milk or formula and stirring over heat until sauce is thickened. Chop brains into small pieces, then add to sauce.

76

VEAL

VEAL AND TOMATOES
8 months

1 small veal cutlet (suitable for
  schnitzel)
1 very ripe tomato, peeled and chopped
1/2 cup Chicken or Beef Stock (see pages
  66 and 78) or water

Slice cutlet into strips and simmer with tomato in stock until tender, about 20
minutes. For young babies, purée cutlet, tomato, and enough cooking liquid
in a blender to make a smooth mixture; older babies enjoy eating the tender
strips as finger food.

LEMON VEAL
12 months

1 small veal cutlet, cut into strips
juice of 1/4 lemon
a little butter or margarine

Sauté veal in butter for a few minutes on each side, sprinkling with lemon
juice while cooking. When meat changes from pink to a gray color it is
cooked.

VEAL CUTLET IN WHEAT GERM
15 months

Great for the whole family—especially delicious cold for packed lunches.

1 lb. veal cutlet (suitable for schnitzel)   wheat germ
whole wheat flour   oil
1 egg beaten with a little milk   lemon juice

Pound veal until thin. Dip into flour, then egg, then coat thoroughly with
wheat germ. Heat oil in frying pan; sauté cutlet until tender, about 5 minutes
each side. Sprinkle with lemon juice before serving. Slice cutlet into strips for
toddlers.

BEEF AND LAMB

Beef and lamb are the last meats to be introduced to a baby because they are tougher and harder to digest than white meats. When first serving beef or lamb, make sure it is thoroughly cooked then puréed to give it a smooth texture. When preparing roasts for the family, reserve a few slices for the baby and purée them with beef stock. Or broil an extra chop, remove all fat and bone, and purée the meat with stock or leftover vegetable water.

A large chop or steak bone makes a wonderful teething aid for an uncomfortable baby.

BEEF STOCK

1 shank bone
4 cups water
1 teaspoon salt (see Note below)
1 carrot, diced
1 onion, chopped (see Note below)
1 small turnip, diced
2 tablespoons chopped parsley
2 stalks celery, chopped
celery leaves

Cut the meat from the bone, and remove any fat. Chop meat into small pieces, and place bone, meat, water and salt in saucepan. Bring slowly to simmering point. Add vegetables, simmer very slowly for 2 to 3 hours in tightly covered saucepan. Remove bones. Cool, skim off any fat. Pour stock through a fine sieve or cheesecloth to strain.

Keep stock in a covered jar in refrigerator, ready for adding to meat, for baby's purée, or for making soups. Freeze a quantity of stock in ice cube trays for a continuous supply.

Note: If using the stock for very young babies, leave out the onion and salt.

BEEF STEW
8 months

1 lb. stewing beef, cubed
2 carrots, scraped and sliced
1 stalk celery, chopped
½ cup peas
2 cups Beef Stock, or leftover vegetable
*   liquid*
sprig or two of parsley
2 tomatoes, peeled and chopped
1 large potato, peeled and quartered

Place all ingredients in a tightly covered saucepan and simmer very gently until meat is so tender it is falling apart, about 1½ hours. Serve to the older members of the family as it is. For baby, remove meat and vegetables and purée either together or separately with enough cooking liquid to make a smooth mixture.

This stew may be varied by adding different vegetables, such as sweet potato, zucchini and green beans, or by adding ¼ cup barley or brown rice. Quantities may be doubled and portions frozen.

MEATBALLS
10–12 months

1 lb. lean ground beef
1 tablespoon chopped parsley
1 egg, beaten
½ cup wheat germ (or whole wheat
*   bread crumbs)*
1 apple, grated

Combine all ingredients and shape into small balls. Broil until cooked. Serve with homemade Tomato Sauce, or hand the meatballs to the baby to manage on his or her own—ideal finger food!

MEAT PIE

12–14 months

1 lb. lean ground beef
2 tablespoons oil
½ cup Beef Stock
2 carrots, cooked and diced
1 cup mashed potato
1 tablespoon wheat germ

Sauté meat in oil until brown; drain carefully. Place meat and stock and carrots in a buttered casserole, top with mashed potato, and sprinkle over wheat germ. Bake in a moderate oven for 15 minutes or until top is brown.

BEEF AND RICE CASSEROLE

18 months

1 lb. lean ground beef
1 medium onion, chopped
1 tablespoon oil
½ cup natural brown rice
¼ teaspoon pepper
sprig fresh thyme
sprig parsley
½ cup raisins
2 cups tomato juice

Brown beef and onion in oil, drain, add remaining ingredients, and mix. Pour into casserole. Cover and bake at 350°F for 30–40 minutes or until all liquid is absorbed.

FILLED PANCAKES

Savory pancakes make an easy, economical, and nutritious meal for the whole family. They freeze well, so make up large quantities and freeze in small quantities for later use. Starting with the Basic Pancake Mixture, make up enough pancakes for a family meal, allowing two to three each for adults and hungry children and one each for the younger children. Spread with savory filling, roll up and place in greased ovenproof dish. Cover with foil and heat through.

A good way to prevent pancakes from drying out while reheating completely, or just warming up, is to dot them with butter or margarine before covering with foil, or use grated cheese and butter, or a small quantity of white or cheese sauce. Even a good splash of homemade Tomato Sauce adds delicious flavor and keeps pancakes moist.

Basic Pancake Mixture
2 years

1 cup whole wheat flour
1 egg
pinch salt
1 1/4 cups milk

Place all ingredients in a blender; blend well. Allow to stand for 1 hour. Remember, pancakes should be very thin, so if the mixture doesn't pour like cream, add more milk, and blend.

To make pancakes without a blender, sift flour and salt into a bowl, add whole egg; mix well. Gradually add milk, beating continuously. Let stand for 1 hour.

Spray frying pan with cooking spray or oil lightly; then melt a little butter in it. Pour in small quantity of mixture, 2–3 tablespoons, tilting pan so that mixture spreads thinly over. When bubbles form, turn over and lightly brown the other side.

Suggested Fillings
Chopped, steamed chicken in parsley sauce—or use leftover pieces of roast
    chicken

Tuna in cheese sauce
Ground meat in Tomato Sauce—homemade, of course!
Any leftover roast meats, cut up and mixed with Tomato Sauce
Steamed fish, flaked and mixed with white sauce plus cheese or parsley
Leftover vegetables mixed with cheese sauce

Use your imagination. Add fresh, chopped herbs, if your children like them; crisp, crumbled bacon for flavor; in fact, anything at all! (Also see Dessert Pancakes on page 90.)

9
HONEY AND SPICE
AND
ALL THINGS NICE!

Desserts and snacks needn't be nutritionless fillers—here are some
health- and vitality-giving delights babies and children will love

DESSERTS

Desserts for the very young can be made simply using yogurt, fresh fruit or fruit juice, stewed fruit, homemade custards, and as the baby gets older, homemade ice cream.

Avoid giving babies and children sweet cakes and cookies. Apart from being "empty," almost nutritionless foods, they destroy a child's appetite for more wholesome food. Fresh fruit, pieces of cheese, celery and carrot sticks, and dried fruit all make healthful snacks.

BANANA PUDDING
7 months

2 very ripe bananas, mashed
½ cup unsweetened Applesauce, or
*   Raw Apple Purée*
1 teaspoon honey

Mix ingredients together, stir till smooth, and chill. Sprinkle with a little cinnamon and wheat germ before serving.

OLD-FASHIONED BAKED CUSTARD
8 months

1 egg (see Note below)
1 teaspoon honey, warmed
1 cup milk
2–3 drops vanilla extract (if using for
*   whole family)*

Butter a small ovenproof dish. Beat the egg and honey together; add milk and vanilla. Pour into dish. Place dish in a baking pan half full of water; this prevents the custard from curdling while it is cooking. Bake in a slow oven at 300–325°F for 15–20 minutes, or until set.
Note: Use only egg yolk when serving to babies under 12 months.

ORANGE BANANAS
8 months

This dessert is delicious for adults when a splash or two of dry sherry is added to the orange juice.

6 firm bananas
juice of 6 oranges
2 tablespoons brown sugar or honey
½ teaspoon cinnamon (optional)

Slice bananas lengthwise; place in ovenproof dish. Cover with orange juice, sprinkle over sugar or honey and cinnamon. Bake in a moderate oven until bananas are soft but not falling apart.

APPLE CUSTARD
8 months

1 red apple
1 teaspoon honey
1 egg (see Note below)

Preheat oven to 350°F. Wash, peel, and core apple, and cut into very thin slices. Place in a well-buttered ovenproof dish. Drizzle over honey. Beat the egg till light and frothy and pour over apple. Bake in slow oven for 30 minutes, or until set.

Note: Use only egg yolk when serving to babies under 12 months.

YOGURT SHERBET
10 months

1 cup Homemade Yogurt
1 cup fresh fruit, cut into very small
*   pieces*

Mix yogurt and fruit together, then freeze for 1 hour.

HONEYED FRUIT

12 months

Use any fresh fruit in season.

Berries, especially currants, are delicious prepared this way but should not be served to babies under 12 months. Place the fruit in a saucepan and cover with cold water. Sweeten to taste with honey, and bring slowly to a boil. Serve immediately.

FRUIT SHERBET

12 months

This can be made using individual ice pop molds, or use an ice cube tray.

2 cups fruit, well blended or mashed to
* a pulp*
2 tablespoons honey
juice of 2 lemons
2 well beaten egg whites

Mix fruit pulp with honey, and add lemon juice. Freeze until just set, then remove from freezer and blend in stiffly beaten egg whites. Freeze.

ICE CREAM

12 months

3 tablespoons granulated sugar
1 teaspoon unflavored gelatin
2 tablespoons water
1 egg
1 tall can evaporated milk
1 teaspoon vanilla extract

Set refrigerator at coldest point. Combine sugar, gelatin, and water in a saucepan and stir over low heat until dissolved, then remove from heat. Beat egg well, and whip evaporated milk until thick. Add beaten egg and mix well. Gradually beat in the sugar-gelatin syrup and flavor with vanilla. Pour into trays and freeze.

FRUITY FROTH
12 months

1 level tablespoon unflavored gelatin
¼ cup water
½ cup hot fruit juice
2 tablespoons honey
1 teaspoon lemon juice
½ cup any fruit pulp, fresh or stewed
1 egg white

Soak gelatin in water; add hot fruit juice. Add honey and lemon juice; stir till honey is dissolved. Cool a little and when mixture is beginning to set, add fruit pulp and beat until mixture is frothy and thick. Fold in stiffly beaten egg white. Pile into serving dish or individual dishes.

CHEESY FREEZE
15 months

4 tablespoons cottage cheese
2 red apples, peeled and cored
½ cup any fruit juice

Blend all ingredients in a blender until smooth. If not using a blender, grate apple finely and mix ingredients thoroughly. Pour into a freezer tray or individual paper cups. Freeze for 30 minutes, then serve.

BERRY ICE CREAM
18 months

1 quart basket ripe strawberries, or the
approximate equivalent weight of
any other fresh berries
⅓ cup water
2 tablespoons honey
pinch salt
juice of ½ lemon
½ cup heavy cream, whipped

Mash berries thoroughly. Combine water, honey, lemon juice and salt, mix thoroughly and add to the mashed berries. Fold in the whipped cream, pour into freezer trays and freeze, stirring occasionally.

FRUITY ICE CREAM

2 years

1 tall can evaporated milk
1 egg
2 tablespoons granulated sugar
1 teaspoon vanilla extract

1 teaspoon gelatin
1 tablespoon boiling water
1 banana, well mashed
2 peaches, ripened and mashed

Pour evaporated milk and well-beaten egg into a bowl. Stir in sugar and vanilla. Dissolve gelatin in boiling water and while still hot, stir into milk. Pour into freezer trays and freeze until very cold. Remove from trays, turn mixture into a chilled bowl, add mashed banana and peaches, and beat until smooth and increased in volume. Return mixture to trays and freeze rapidly.

APPLE CRUMBLE

2 years

6 Granny Smith apples, peeled, cored
   and sliced
3–4 tablespoons honey
4 tablespoons butter or margarine
1 cup whole wheat flour

2 tablespoons wheat germ
pinch of salt
1 teaspoon cinnamon (optional)
4 tablespoons raw sugar

Butter a baking dish. Place layers of sliced apple in dish; drizzle over the honey. Mix together butter, flour, wheat germ, salt, cinnamon and sugar until mixture resembles bread crumbs. Sprinkle over the apples and bake at 375°F for 30 minutes.

APRICOT FLUFF

2 years

Children love this apricot fluff, and dressed up with almonds and whipped cream it makes a special dinner party dessert.

3/4 cup purée of dried apricots
4 tablespoons raw sugar
5 egg whites, stiffly beaten

slivered almonds (not for children
   under 4)

Soak apricots overnight in water to cover, then purée until smooth. Add sugar, then fold in stiffly beaten egg whites, place in a casserole, and sprinkle with almonds. Bake in a moderate oven for 45 to 50 minutes.

SPICY RICE

2 years

2 cups natural brown rice
1 tablespoon grated orange rind
2 teaspoons grated lemon rind
  (optional)
2 tablespoons butter or margarine
3 tablespoons honey
juice of 2 oranges
1 cup stewed fruit or well drained
  canned fruit

1 tablespoon raisins
1/2 cup evaporated milk
3 tablespoons brown sugar
1/2 teaspoon cinnamon
1/2 teaspoon nutmeg
a little extra butter

Place rice in ovenproof saucepan with grated rinds, butter and 1 tablespoon honey. Measure orange juice with enough water to make 4 cups; add to rice. Cover and cook gently on stove until rice is tender and all liquid is absorbed. Remove from heat and stir in fruit, 2 tablespoons honey, raisins and milk. Sprinkle surface of rice with brown sugar and mixed spices. Dot with butter and bake in a moderate oven until topping is melted.

DESSERT PANCAKES

Pancakes are usually great favorites for the whole family. Prepared in advance, they can be frozen and warmed up when needed—great time-savers! (Dessert pancakes are usually served with sweet fillings, but don't overlook their usefulness as an economical main course.)

Basic Pancake Mixture
1 cup whole wheat flour
pinch salt
1 egg
1 1/4 cups milk
butter

Place all ingredients in blender; blend well. Allow to stand for 1 hour. If mixture doesn't pour like cream, add more milk and blend again.

If you are not using a blender, sift the flour and salt into a bowl, add whole egg, and mix well. Gradually add milk, beating continuously. Stand mixture aside for 1 hour.

Spray frying pan with cooking spray or oil lightly; melt a little butter in it.

Pour in small quantity of mixture, tilting pan so that mixture spreads thinly over. When bubbles form, turn over and brown the other side.

Try some of the following fillings:
lemon juice and honey or sugar
stewed apple and raisins
stewed apple and plain yogurt
stewed apple and cottage cheese
cream cheese beaten with raisins and honey
stewed apricots and sour cream
any fresh fruit purée (berries are delicious)
orange juice and honey or sugar

Try rolling a pancake around a whole peeled banana which has been warmed in the oven. Secure it with a toothpick and top with a sauce made with lemon juice and honey—delicious!

MUNCHIES, CRUNCHIES, AND SLURPS— treats full of flavor and nutrition!

Avoid giving young children sweets for as long as possible, but sooner or later they will learn the magic word and naturally will be offered some sugary delight by a friend, neighbor or doting relative. The answer? Make your own—making them is fun, easy and a great indoor activity for the under-fives who are bored with their usual play.

YUMMIES

½ cup butter	*½ cup coconut*
½ cup honey	*½ cup raisins or chopped dates*
½ cup milk	*½ cup wheat germ*
½ cup raw peanuts (see Note below)	*½ cup mashed, cooked egg yolk*

Melt butter and honey over gentle heat in saucepan. Add the remaining ingredients and stir well. If the mixture is too thin, add more chopped fruit or nuts, or a sprinkle of dried milk. Pour mixture into greased shallow container and chill well. When set, cut into squares.

Note: Cookies containing whole or chopped nuts should not be given to children under 4 years. Grind nuts fine in the blender or food processor before adding to mixture.

SESAME SEED SQUARES

4 tablespoons honey
4 tablespoons Peanut Butter
¼ cup nonfat dry milk
4 tablespoons shredded coconut
  (fresh is best)
4 tablespoons chopped raisins
¼ cup sesame seeds

Heat honey and peanut butter in a saucepan over gentle heat. Add nonfat dry milk, coconut, raisins, then seeds. Mix thoroughly. Press into shallow container, refrigerate until firm. Cut into squares.

HEALTH BARS

4 oz. dates	2 tablespoons raisins
8 oz. dried figs	2 tablespoons golden raisins
4 oz. chopped walnuts (grind these fine	8 oz. dried apricots
for the very young)	1 teaspoon grated lemon rind

Grind all ingredients except lemon rind in a blender or food processor. Mix together thoroughly, then press into a well buttered shallow container. Cut into bars and roll in lemon rind.

PEANUT BALLS

4 tablespoons Peanut Butter	2 tablespoons honey
(homemade is best)	½ teaspoon nutmeg
2 tablespoons water	coconut—freshly grated is definitely
2 tablespoons instant nonfat dry milk	best!

In a small saucepan, mix all ingredients except coconut. Stir over low heat until mixture is very thick. Remove from heat and stir in enough coconut to bind the mixture together well enough to be formed into balls. Roll into small balls and then into more coconut. Chill.

FRUIT AND NUT BALLS

1 cup water
1 cup dried apricots
½ cup ground almonds
½ cup chopped dates
4 tablespoons honey
½ cup wheat germ
½ cup golden raisins
½ cup shredded coconut
2 teaspoons carob powder (see page 22)
sesame seeds (optional)

Place apricots and water in a saucepan, bring to a boil; simmer gently till apricots are tender. Remove from heat, add remaining ingredients except sesame seeds, mix well, and cool. Roll mixture into small balls, then into extra coconut or sesame seeds if you wish. Refrigerate till well hardened.

ICE POPS—delicious frozen treats on sticks

Homemade ice pops are great for children who are sick and won't eat any solid food and are especially delicious for children with sore throats! You can buy special freezer trays for making your own ice pops, and any supermarket stocks the little sticks to put into the treats just before they freeze solid.

Try some of the following combinations:

milk with carob powder (see page 22)—1 teaspoon carob powder to 1 cup
    milk
milk plus egg yolk and honey
milk plus shredded coconut
milk with grated apple
Yogurt plus fresh fruit purée
Yogurt plus fruit juice—equal parts
apple juice with tiny green grapes (not for the under-ones)
milk blended with chopped nuts (ground for the very young)
Yogurt with chopped dried fruit and honey
fresh fruit juice plus fruit purée—equal parts
equal parts Homemade Ice Cream and fresh fruit purée

COOKIES

Children love cookies, but try to avoid the white sugar commercial variety that provide empty calories and rot small teeth. Homemade cookies are delicious and simple to make. Make a double batch and freeze half.

OAT CRISPIES

½ cup whole wheat flour
1 teaspoon baking powder
1¼ cups rolled oats
6 tablespoons butter
2 tablespoons honey
¼ cup milk
raisins

Preheat oven to 400°F. Sift flour and baking powder; add rolled oats. Rub in butter; mix thoroughly. Add honey and milk; mix well. Chill mixture for 30 minutes. Roll teaspoonfuls of mixture into balls, then flatten with a fork and place on well oiled cookie sheets. Top each with a raisin and bake for 15–20 minutes, or until golden brown.

DATE COOKIES

½ lb. butter
1 cup raw sugar
1 egg, beaten
¾ cup dates, chopped
grated rind of ½ orange
¾ cup walnuts (ground for young
   children)
2 cups whole wheat flour

2 teaspoons cinnamon
pinch nutmeg or allspice
½ teaspoon baking soda

Cream butter and sugar, add the egg, then the dates, rind and walnuts. Mix well. Add flour and spices, then baking soda dissolved in 1 teaspoon of water. Mix together well. Drop in spoonfuls onto cookie sheet and bake at 300°F for 20 minutes.

OATMEAL MUNCHIES

½ cup butter or margarine
½ cup raw sugar
1 egg
1 tablespoon orange juice
3 tablespoons milk
1 cup oatmeal
1 cup whole wheat flour
1¼ teaspoons baking powder
pinch salt
1 cup golden raisins
1 teaspoon cinnamon

Cream butter and sugar, add beaten egg, then orange juice and milk. Mix dry ingredients together, gradually add to butter and sugar mixture, and mix thoroughly. Place teaspoonfuls onto greased cookie sheet and bake for 10–15 minutes in a moderate oven.

CARROT COOKIES

½ lb. butter or margarine
¾ cup raw sugar
1 egg
1 teaspoon vanilla extract
2 cups whole wheat flour
pinch salt
2 teaspoons baking powder
2 cups grated raw carrot
¼ cup chopped or ground peanuts
   (raw)
¼ cup wheat germ
1 teaspoon cinnamon
2 teaspoons grated orange rind

Cream butter and sugar, add egg and vanilla and beat well. Sift flour, salt, and baking powder, and add with carrots, nuts, wheat germ, cinnamon and orange rind until combined. Place teaspoonfuls of mixture onto a greased cookie sheet. Bake in moderate oven for 20–25 minutes.

CRUNCHY COOKIES

¼ *lb. butter*
1½ *cups raw sugar*
1 *egg*
1 *teaspoon cinnamon*
½ *cup toasted sesame seeds*
½ *cup raisins*
1 *cup whole wheat flour*
walnut pieces (not for younger
  children)

Cream the butter and sugar, add the egg and mix well. Add remaining ingredients except walnut pieces and mix well. Spread the mixture into a well greased jelly roll pan, sprinkle with walnut pieces (or coconut) and bake in a moderate oven for 20 minutes. When cool, cut into squares.

PEANUT TREATS

¼ *lb. butter or margarine*
½ *cup raw sugar*
1 *egg*
1½ *cups self-rising whole wheat flour*
2 *teaspoons carob powder (see page 22)*
½ *cup raw peanuts (see Note below)*

Cream butter and sugar, add egg, and beat well. Mix in sifted flour, carob powder and peanuts. Place teaspoonfuls onto greased cookie sheet. Bake in moderate oven for 12–15 minutes.
Note: Cookies containing whole or chopped nuts should not be given to children under 4 years. Grind nuts in blender before adding to mixture.

BANANA GOODIES

3/4 cup butter
1 cup brown sugar
1 egg, beaten
1 1/2 cups whole wheat flour
1/2 teaspoon baking soda
1/2 teaspoon salt
1 teaspoon cinnamon
1/2 teaspoon nutmeg
1 cup mashed banana
1 3/4 cups oatmeal

Cream butter and sugar, add beaten egg and mix well. Mix flour, baking soda, salt and spices together, add to creamed mixture and mix well. Add banana and oatmeal. Mix thoroughly. Place teaspoonfuls onto a greased cookie sheet and bake at 400°F for 12–15 minutes.

Any extras you like may be added to these cookies, e.g., raisins, chopped (ground for the under-4s) nuts and grated orange peel.

10
PARTY FOOD

Party food can be a sheer delight to look at and eat, as well as being
nutritious

The main thing to keep in mind when preparing parties for the under-fives is to keep the food simple, easy to eat and not too rich! There really is no need for an elaborate smorgasbord for small children; they will be delighted with their old, tried and true favorites. Try homemade ice cream scooped into cones and dipped in ground nuts or chopped raisins, jellies made from fruit juice set in molds and decorated with slices of fresh fruit, a few cupcakes and cookies and special party sandwiches. Don't forget to decorate the table with baskets of homemade candies, popcorn, carrot and celery sticks, and even chunks of cheese on toothpicks stuck into oranges to make porcupines. Drinks can be homemade orangeade or lemonade, pure fruit juices or milk. Keep the birthday cake light and simple—it will probably be judged on the vividness of its icing anyway!

FUNNY FACE COOKIES

1 cup butter   *1 cup arrowroot*
1 cup sugar   *1 teaspoon cream of tartar*
3 eggs   *1/2 teaspoon baking soda*
3 cups plain flour   *pinch salt*

These cookies, with their delicious creamy topping and funny faces, help to make the party table look bright and attractive.

Cream butter and sugar, add eggs one at a time; beat well. Add flour and arrowroot, cream of tartar, soda and salt; mix well. Place teaspoonfuls onto greased cookie sheet, press down with bottom of a glass to make flat, then cut with an oval cookie cutter.

Bake cookies in a moderate oven 10–15 minutes till pale golden color. Allow to cool completely, then ice with Honey and Cream Cheese Icing. Decorate faces with raisins for eyes, and jelly beans for nose and mouth.

Honey and Cream Cheese Icing
8 oz. cream cheese
1–2 tablespoons honey (more or less to
taste)

Place cheese and honey in a blender and blend till smooth.

This makes a delicious icing for all types of cakes and cookies; it is also good as a filling for cakes and slices. Vary basic icing with chopped or ground nuts or raisins, prunes or chopped apricots.

RAISIN CUPCAKES

Cupcakes are always popular with tiny children. They love to peel off the paper! Also, you will have less mess than if children have to manage larger pieces of sliced cake. Try putting a candle on a cupcake for each child guest instead of the traditional large birthday cake.

1/4 lb. butter

3/4 cup sugar

a few drops vanilla extract

2 eggs

2 cups self-rising flour

1/2 cup golden raisins

1/2 cup milk

Cream butter, sugar and vanilla. Beat eggs then add gradually and mix well. Mix raisins with flour, add flour and milk alternately to mixture, and mix well. Spoon into approximately 25 paper baking cups. Bake in a moderate oven 20–35 minutes.

GINGERBREAD MEN

Instead of sending each child home with a loot bag of candy, try wrapping gingerbread men in clear plastic wrap, tying each with ribbon and giving them to the children as they leave. A really effective touch would be to pipe each child's name on a gingerbread man in white icing, if you have the time!

1 1/4 cups raw sugar

1/2 cup honey

2 tablespoons butter

1 tablespoon grated lemon rind

1 tablespoon lemon juice

1 egg

1 1/2 cups flour

1 teaspoon each salt and baking
powder

1/2 teaspoon each cinnamon and nutmeg

1–1 1/2 teaspoons of ground ginger

To decorate—golden raisins, white
icing

Place raw sugar, honey, butter, lemon rind and juice in a saucepan, and stir over low heat until combined. Cool, then mix in egg. Sift dry ingredients into a bowl and add liquid mixture—knead into a soft dough. Roll on a lightly floured board to 1-inch thickness and cut into gingerbread man shapes. Place onto cookie sheets, decorate with raisins for eyes, nose, buttons, etc., and bake at 325°F for 15 minutes. Remove from sheets while warm; let cool, then decorate with white icing.

BUTTERED POPCORN

Popcorn is a great favorite with the over-threes, and it is an economical way to delight small guests and decorate the birthday table. Popcorn can be plain or colored, placed on the table in bowls or cups, tied in twists of colored cellophane as a going-home gift, or used to decorate the birthday cake.

1/2 cup unpopped corn
2 tablespoons oil

Heat oil in a large saucepan until very hot. Add corn, put a lid on saucepan; shake over heat until popping ceases. Place popped corn into a bowl, dot with butter and sprinkle with salt.

BRAN MUFFINS

1 cup milk
2 tablespoons molasses
1 teaspoon baking soda
2 cups 100% bran cereal

1 cup whole wheat flour
1/2–1 cup golden raisins or currants or
  chopped raisins or dates
1 tablespoon oil or melted butter

Warm milk and molasses slightly and add soda. The instant it froths, add dry ingredients. Stir in chosen fruit and oil or butter. Place in spoonfuls in greased muffin tins and bake at 350°F for 15–20 minutes.

APRICOT BARS

3/4 cup finely chopped dried apricots
1/2 cup water
1/3 cup finely chopped almonds (ground
  for younger children)
1 teaspoon lemon juice
1 teaspoon orange juice

1/2 cup honey
1 cup nonfat dry milk
1 tablespoon wheat germ
1/2 cup golden raisins
1/2 cup shredded coconut

Apricot bars wrapped in colorful cellophane and placed in little baskets on the table look delicious!

   Combine apricots and water in a saucepan, bring to a boil, and simmer till just tender. Remove from heat, add remaining ingredients, and mix thoroughly. Spread mixture into lightly greased (cooking spray is best) shallow pan. Refrigerate for several hours before cutting into bars.

CANDIED POPCORN

½ cup unpopped corn
2 tablespoons oil
2 cups sugar
1 cup water
½ teaspoon food coloring

Heat oil in large saucepan until very hot, add corn, cover and shake over heat until popping ceases. Remove from heat; place popcorn in a bowl to cool.

Put sugar, water and food coloring in a large saucepan; stir over low heat until sugar dissolves. Bring to a boil; simmer uncovered until a drop or two of the toffee sets in cold water. Remove from heat. Pour popcorn into toffee, stir constantly until toffee thoroughly coats popcorn and remove from pan and cool. A large tray is best for cooling.

PARTY MICE

Small children love to find these little mice scattered over the party table. Use pitted prunes for the babies, press pieces of jelly beans on for eyes and thin strips of licorice stuck on with pieces of toothpick for ears and tails.

ORANGE FLUFF

Enjoyed by the fours and fives.

2½ cups fresh orange juice—reserve
*   halved orange shells*
1 tablespoon unflavored gelatin
2 tablespoons honey
2 eggs, separated

Place orange juice in a bowl, sprinkle over gelatin, and let stand for 30 minutes. Heat orange juice and honey together gently in a saucepan. Just before the boiling point is reached, remove from heat and pour into well beaten egg yolks, stirring continuously. Leave to cool. Beat egg whites till stiff and fold into cooled orange mixture. Pile orange fluff into orange halves which have been carefully scraped to remove remaining orange pulp, and place in refrigerator to set.

GELATIN ORANGES

Reserve halved orange shells when using the pulp or juice, until you have enough for at least one half per guest. Make sure there are no holes in the shells and then place them on a tray. Make up two or three different-colored gelatins and carefully pour these into the shells. Refrigerate until set. Just before serving, cut each half into two (or three with large oranges) and arrange the wedges attractively on a platter.

BANANA CAKE

¼ lb. butter
½ cup sugar
2 eggs
1 cup, plus 2 tablespoons self-rising
  wheat flour
3 small ripe bananas
1 teaspoon baking soda
1 teaspoon vanilla extract
1 tablespoon milk

Cream butter and sugar, add eggs and beat well. Add mashed bananas. Dissolve soda in vanilla and milk. Add flour and milk alternately, mixing well. Pour mixture into prepared cake pan and bake in a moderate oven for 30 minutes or until done. Cool, then ice with caramel icing.

Caramel Icing
1 cup brown sugar
1½ teaspoons butter
¼ cup milk

Place all ingredients in a saucepan, and stir until mixture boils. Simmer 5 minutes without stirring. Beat until thick enough to spread.

As well as the sweet treats, make sure you have plenty of savory food to offer, too: carrot and celery sticks, small bowls of raisins, cheese chunks and tiny whole wheat bread sandwiches.

PARTY SANDWICHES

Trim slices of whole wheat bread by cutting off crusts. Spread with butter or margarine, then top with hard-cooked egg or tuna mashed with mayonnaise. Don't spread too much filling onto bread or it will be too difficult for small children to manage. Now decorate the open sandwich to make faces or designs with grated carrot, raisins, cheese sticks, tiny wedges of tomato, etc.

11
LUNCH IDEAS FOR THE PRESCHOOLERS

It is important to keep lunches for small children who will be eating without your supervision very simple, but attractive and fresh

It is a very exciting time when small children go off for their first day at preschool or kindergarten. Their days will be packed with busy activity and new things to see and do. Eating will probably be the last thing on their minds—it will interfere too much with chatter and play! However, without a healthy, vitality-giving lunch, youthful energy will fade and it will be a tired, sulking child who greets you in the afternoon. Help your children to maintain daylong energy and happiness by providing easy-to-eat, appealing and nourishing lunch and morning snack foods.

SANDWICHES

Sandwiches are a good lunch for most youngsters as they are easy to manage and quick to eat with a minimum of mess! Use only whole wheat, rye or mixed-grain breads and vary them occasionally. Sandwich fillings should be based on protein such as egg, meat, fish, cheese, soybeans or nuts, with milk or fruit juice and fresh fruit to follow.

Try some of these sandwich-filling suggestions.

PEANUT BUTTER

Peanut butter is usually a great favorite in homes where there are young children. Try making your own—it's fun, and the homemade product is delicious. Buy raw, unsalted peanuts from your health food store; 1 lb. will make quite a large quantity of peanut butter. Of course, you can buy peanuts in the shell and older children will enjoy helping you shell and skin them—a great rainy-day indoor activity! Place the shelled, skinned nuts into a blender, a small quantity at a time, with a drizzle of good quality cooking oil, and blend till smooth. Keep adding nuts and oil until completely blended. You will need approximately 1–2 tablespoons of oil for 1 lb. of nuts. If the older children prefer their peanut butter crunchy, just chop a small quantity of nuts in the blender, and stir into the smooth peanut butter. Store the peanut butter in a screw-top jar in your refrigerator.

Try peanut butter with the following:
chopped raisins
grated carrot and ground nuts moistened with a little mayonnaise
grated apple and chopped raisins
sliced banana (sprinkle with lemon juice to prevent discoloring)
finely grated cabbage and carrot

Nut butters can be made with other nuts also; almond butter is expensive but delicious as a special treat; or try walnut butter, cashew butter or macadamia butter—delicious!

CHEESE

Cream cheese blended with:

fresh fruit purée
ground raisins (just place cheese and raisins together in blender and blend)
grated carrot and ground nuts

Cottage cheese with:

grated carrot and ground raisins
grated hard-cooked egg
chopped parsley
finely chopped pineapple
grated apple (sprinkle with lemon juice first)
sliced mild cheddar cheese with tomato
grated cheddar cheese with finely chopped celery or carrot moistened with a
    little mayonnaise

EGG

Chopped or mashed hard-cooked egg with the following:
mashed sardines
shredded lettuce
crumbled, crispy bacon
grated carrot

FISH

Drained canned tuna or salmon with the following:
Mayonnaise and chopped hard-cooked egg
lemon juice and grated carrot
Mayonnaise and chopped parsley
Mayonnaise and chopped celery

MEAT

Cooked meat should be chopped very finely for young children and moistened with a little mayonnaise or milk to keep it together. Use chicken, lamb or beef on their own or mix with some of the following:
unsweetened Applesauce
sliced tomato
fruit chutney
finely grated carrot or celery

SOYBEAN SPREAD

Soybean spread is a nutritious and very economical sandwich filling. You can use it on its own, or top it with tuna, chopped hard-cooked egg and parsley, or grated cheese.

1 cup soybeans
1 slice bacon, finely chopped
1 onion, finely chopped
1 clove garlic (optional)
4 tablespoons fresh chopped parsley
¾ cup Mayonnaise
1½ teaspoons soy sauce
pinch salt, freshly ground black pepper
    to taste

Cook the soybeans until tender (see recipe in Dried Beans and Lentils section). When tender, mash thoroughly with remaining cooking liquid. Sauté the bacon for a few minutes, then add onion, garlic if using, and parsley, and sauté until onion is soft and golden. Mix onion and parsley with soybean mixture, then add remaining ingredients. Mix together thoroughly. You may need a little more mayonnaise to get the right spreading consistency. Store in a screw-top jar in the refrigerator.

Experiment with this basic recipe. You may decide to add fresh or dried herbs if your children like them, or chopped fresh green or red pepper, or grated celery.

MAYONNAISE

Make you own mayonnaise; it's quick, very simple, and economical. This recipe makes a bland mayonnaise well liked by children. The addition of garlic and herbs and English or German mustard produces a mayonnaise with more tang.

2 egg yolks
pinch salt, pepper to taste
1½ teaspoons French mustard
1½ teaspoons white vinegar
1 cup polyunsaturated oil
optional: 1–2 cloves garlic, English or
   German mustard, fresh herbs

Place egg yolks in blender or clean, dry bowl. Blend at high speed or whisk until thick, then add seasonings and vinegar. Blend at high speed for 10 seconds. Then, at highest speed, slowly but continuously pour in the oil.

OTHER LUNCH IDEAS

Munching Chicken (see recipe in Chicken section)
Pieces of Veal in Wheat Germ (see recipe in Veal section)
Raw carrot and celery sticks
Small boxes of raisins
Sticks of cheese
Humpty Dumpties (see recipe in Egg section)
Fresh vegetable and brown rice salad, stored in a tight-sealing container, for older children
Salad of hard-cooked eggs, tomato wedges and meat slices in a sealed container, for older children

For a change, instead of including bread in your children's lunches, try offering a Cheese Scone to go with a little salad.

CHEESE SCONES

2 cups white self-rising flour
1½ cups whole wheat flour
2½ teaspoons baking powder
6 tablespoons butter
1 cup grated cheese
1–1½ cups milk soured with a few
  drops of lemon juice
pinch salt

Preheat oven to hot—425°F. Mix flours, baking powder and salt in a large mixing bowl. Rub in butter until mixture resembles bread crumbs. Mix in cheese. Make a well in the center and add enough soured milk to make a soft dough. Turn onto a floured board and knead gently. Press out to ¾-inch thickness, and cut into rounds. Place on well buttered baking sheet, brush with milk and bake in hot oven for approximately 12 minutes.

Homemade cookies can also be included in lunches occasionally for a treat, or a piece of health bar for a surprise. Usually, however, a piece of fruit such as a peeled and sectioned orange in an airtight container, or a small apple or banana, is enough to finish the meal. In the summer, try placing the children's plastic drink containers of juice or milk in the freezer overnight so that drinks will be more refreshing the next day.

Another good idea for summer lunches is a sealed container of homemade fruit yogurt which has been frozen overnight. By lunchtime the yogurt will have thawed but will still be cold and fresh.

Midmorning snacks are best kept very simple—a stick or two of cheese, a small apple or banana, a pack of raisins. All high-energy foods, these will satisfy a child's hunger and keep him or her going until lunchtime. Do avoid starchy, sugary snacks of cakes, cookies and candies; their energy boost is short lasting and besides, they encourage the formation of teeth cavities!

12
LET'S
PUT IT ALL
TOGETHER

The following is simply a guide to help you plan your baby's day with a minimum of fuss

For your own family you will, of course, have your own ideas about how much food, what food, and when it should be eaten. Your doctor will no doubt help to plan what is best for your individual baby.

4–6 MONTHS

At this very early stage, your baby's main food will, of course, be milk, either breast or bottle. However, somewhere between 4 and 6 months it is a good idea to begin introducing solids, a very little at a time, and very gradually (See Chapter 2). At this time, your baby will probably begin to enjoy fruit purée, plain Yogurt and pureed vegetables.

FIRST MORNING FEED

Breast or bottle milk, then small quantity, according to appetite, of fresh mashed banana and Yogurt.

AROUND MIDDAY

After the breast or bottle feeding, offer baby some Carrot Custard or Butternut Squash Soup. Baked Potato and Apple Pie are also popular, as are plain vegetables puréed.

AT NIGHT

After breast or bottle feed, some Rice Smoothie, Rice Cream, or Banana Oatmeal will satisfy the baby of this age and help him to sleep contentedly all night!

6–9 MONTHS

ON WAKING

Offer baby milk, either breast or bottle. This should keep him happy while you wake and feed the other members of your family.

BREAKFAST

A good breakfast for babies this age could be:

2–5 tablespoons of cooked cereal, e.g., Banana Oatmeal
2 fingers of crisp rye or whole wheat toast and Applesauce
or
1 serving of wheat germ/yogurt breakfast with mashed banana or grated apple
2 fingers of crisp rye or whole wheat toast and Peanut Butter
or
1 hard-cooked egg yolk mashed with half a ripe banana
2 fingers rye or whole wheat toast and butter

If you are a working mother and mornings are unbelievably hectic, try feeding your baby a meal-in-a-bottle breakfast—saves spending precious minutes spooning cereal and fruit into a dawdling baby. Works well for all members of the family actually! Fill a blender with a fruit/egg yolk/milk/wheat germ mixture and blend. Strain mixture into a bottle for baby and pour into glasses for rest of family—breakfast in an instant.

MID-MORNING

Orange juice

LUNCH (or the main meal of the day)

Milk—bottle or breast
Egg yolk, or 2–3 tablespoons of meat or fish
2–3 tablespoons vegetables
2 tablespoons fresh or stewed fruit or milk dessert
Sample menus
Egg in the Nest with Zucchini Slurp
Fresh apple or Applesauce and Baked Custard
or
Cheesy Spinach Potato Pie plus puréed carrot
Orange Bananas
or
Liver Stew with puréed carrot and peas
Apple Custard
or
Steamed Fish with Sweet Potato Custard plus puréed pumpkin
Banana Pudding

MID-AFTERNOON

Fruit juice and a Rusk for very hungry babies

DINNER

A lighter meal than lunch, first bottle or breast milk, then perhaps some vegetable soup in winter and Yogurt and fruit in warmer months.

Sample menus
Butternut Squash Soup
2 fingers whole wheat toast
or
Mashed Banana and Yogurt
or
Pumpkin Pie

9–12 MONTHS

ON WAKING

Breast or bottle milk, or if you prefer, fruit juice at this time and milk with breakfast.

BREAKFAST

Sample Menus
Oatmeal plus Applesauce
Whole wheat toast
or
Wheat germ/Yogurt breakfast with mashed banana
Whole wheat toast
or
Oatmeal with grated apple
Whole wheat toast with Homemade Peanut Butter
or
Cooked egg with crisp toast fingers
Applesauce and Yogurt

MID-MORNING

Fruit juice

LUNCH

Milk, bottle or breast
Meat—2 tablespoons poultry or fish
Vegetables—2 tablespoons
Fresh or cooked fruit and/or milk dessert
Sample Menus
Chicken Stew with Potato Soufflé
Fruity Froth
or
Fish Fingers with mashed or puréed parsnips and carrot
Fruit Sherbert

Alternatively, a good lunch idea for a tired baby of this age would be a fruit/ egg/milk/or juice blend, strained into his bottle or cup—needs far less effort on his part, and a great alternative to canned food if you have had a busy morning or arrived home too late to cook lunch! If your baby has a milk blend for lunch, serve him his meat or egg and vegetables for his evening meal.

MID-AFTERNOON

Fruit juice, ½ banana

DINNER

Milk, breast or bottle
Vegetable soup, either hot or cold
Yogurt and fresh or stewed fruit
Sample Menus
Carrot soup with grated cheese
Whole wheat toast with Homemade Peanut Butter
Fresh or stewed fruit
or
Plain Yogurt with any fresh fruit in season
Whole wheat toast with Homemade Peanut Butter

12–18 MONTHS

Often during this period mothers change their baby's main meal from the middle of the day to the evening. It certainly doesn't matter to the baby—find whichever fits into your day best! The following sample menus for lunch and dinner can of course be changed about. If, however, you find that your baby is too tired to want to eat his main meal in the evening, it would be better to continue serving it for lunch until he is a little older.

ON WAKING

Milk or fruit juice, then milk at breakfast

BREAKFAST

Hot Corn Cereal with Applesauce
½–1 Scrambled Egg
Whole wheat toast
or
Wheat germ/Yogurt breakfast with stewed apricots
½–1 cooked egg
Whole wheat toast with Homemade Nut Butter
or
Oatmeal with mashed banana
½–1 Scrambled Egg
Whole wheat toast and Applesauce

MID-MORNING

Fruit juice, piece of cheese

LUNCH

Plain Yogurt with any fresh or stewed fruit, plus a sprinkling of wheat germ or brewer's yeast
Rusk or whole wheat bread with nut butter or grated cheese
Milk
or

Cold or hot vegetable soup, e.g., Squash Soup with grated cheese
Whole wheat bread with Peanut Butter
Mashed banana and yogurt dessert
Milk
or
Vegetable Bake
Custard and prunes
Whole wheat bread and nut butter or honey
Milk

MID-AFTERNOON

Fruit juice, Rusk and honey

DINNER

Good serving of meat, fish or poultry, e.g., 1 broiled lamb loin chop, 2
    tablespoons ground or puréed meat, plus 2 tablespoons mixed vegetables
Milk pudding with fresh or stewed fruit
Sample Menus
Meat Pie with puréed or mashed potato, carrots and zucchini
Yogurt Apple
Milk
or
Tuna Mornay
Homemade Ice Cream and stewed fruit
Milk
or
Brains in Cream Sauce with puréed spinach and potato
Honeyed Fruit
Milk

18 MONTHS—3 YEARS

ON WAKING

This depends on your toddler; some just can't wait for a bottle or cup of milk or fruit juice, others play happily until breakfast.

BREAKFAST

Around this age most toddlers lose their previous good appetites and often refuse breakfast completely. Experiment till you find something your toddler enjoys, then stick to it until he calls for a change!

Sample Menus
Banana/egg/milk blend with brewer's yeast, strained into a cup or bottle
or
Butter-Fried Egg and whole wheat toast with nut butter or honey
or
Cottage Cheese Pancakes with Applesauce

MID-MORNING

Fruit juice and piece of cheese

LUNCH

Sandwich of whole wheat or mixed-grain bread with Homemade Liver Pâté, grated or cottage cheese with grated carrot, Peanut Butter
Piece of fruit
Milk
or
Plain Homemade Yogurt with fresh or stewed fruit in season
Piece of cheese or grated apple
Milk
or
Hot or cold vegetable soup
Whole wheat bread
Milk

MID-AFTERNOON

Fruit or fruit juice

DINNER

Try to serve your toddler the same food as you are serving the rest of the family; it means far less effort and less temptation to use canned foods.

Sample Menus
The following are really "family" meals, easily adapted to all tastes.

Liver and Bacon Casserole with mashed potatoes and mixed vegetables
Old-fashioned Baked Custard and stewed apricots
Milk
or
Spinach Roll-Ups served with Potato Pancakes
Homemade Ice Cream with fresh banana or any fruit in season
Milk
or
Veal Cutlets in Wheat Germ served with Spinach Soufflé
Spicy Rice
Milk

INDEX